A Note f

There is a generation of men and women alive today who were old enough to remember the Great Depression. They were born long before the first television set. News and information was not at their fingertips, and they did not share their daily thoughts and feelings over a mobile device. Instead, they played on street corners and told each other stories for entertainment. In the prime of their youth, they were cast into the cloud of a global war. They lived through nearly a century of monumental change and progress, tragedy and triumph. They persevered and largely made lives worth living. Their wisdom and experience is a cultural asset that becomes scarcer every day. It should be valued and cherished. It must live on.

This book originated from a conversation at a wedding reception in May 2013. A familial exchange with an older gentleman at my table progressed into a captivating dialogue in which he eloquently shared episodes of growing up in the 1920s and being at war in the 1940s. His portrayals carried me through admiration, laughter, and heartache, and compelled me to volunteer to record them onto these pages for his family, friends, and future generations.

Our initial conversation progressed into hours of recorded interviews, and the examination of his personal memoirs, shoeboxes of wartime letters to loved ones, and dozens of photographs and artifacts from his life. Military records and veteran compilations dated as early as 1941 were thoroughly consulted to verify factual elements and the location and timing of events.

While individual perceptions of complicated incidents are destined to vary from one man to the next, especially on a battlefield, every precaution has been taken to report the given perspective as precisely as possible and without embellishment. Historical context has been provided to the extent necessary with reasoning that a more thorough study of World War II can be found elsewhere. The names of fellow soldiers have been largely omitted out of respect for those men and their families, and once again in recognition that one man's perspective should not forever solidify the record.

In the end, I hope to have cemented in time the experience of sitting across from this representative of a treasured and fleeting generation as he shared some of the most memorable experiences of his life; I hope to have revealed the extent to which extraordinary acts of heroism can be left untold, through the anecdotal biography of an ordinary man who managed to survive time and time again; and I hope to have embodied my sincere respect and admiration for the sacrifices of all veterans past and present. Thank you for your service.

- Steven Attanasio

TABLE OF CONTENTS

CHAPTER ONE

Present Day (2014)

At the midpoint of Long Island on the northern side rests a modest hamlet of seventeen thousand residents known as Kings Park. On a crisp fall afternoon, curving parkways pleasantly reward motorists with surrounding rows of otherwise ordinary trees, now illuminated by leaves of gold, red, and orange. Departing from the Sunken Meadow Parkway, travelers find themselves on a suburban road lined with generously spaced homes and picturesque front yards. Tall wooden poles rising from the ground drape black electrical cables high above the sidewalks and through the hanging leaves. There is a sense of neighborhood and residential life, much quieter and peaceful than the bustling city fifty miles west.

Halfway down a particular street on the left-hand side sits a tranquil two-story house with pale, bluish-green lap siding, home to an elderly couple and one of their two children. The husband is ninety-five years old and his wife is ninety-three years young. Their quaint home is lined with thick comfortable carpeting in the living room and on the stairwell, complimented by large soft couches. There are many photographs of family, friends, and days of old along the walls and on tabletops.

The couple is healthier than the average person many years their junior. Nowadays, the husband wakes up at 7:00 a.m. and goes to bed at 2:00 a.m. He likes to stay up late watching movies that came out in the early 1940s that he never had a chance to see, and silent films from when he was a kid. In the kitchen, his wife is at the hot stove cooking beans and escarole. She has a glass of white wine to the side and moves slowly but deliberately with a smile on her face.

"My wife is a good cook," he says. "How long have we been married, honey?"

"Sixty-seven years!" she replies enthusiastically.

"Oh come on. You're stretching it. It's only been sexty-sex, I mean sixty-six years," he says with his eyebrows raised and a half smile.

They still enjoy entertaining, hosting their children, grandchildren, great-grandchildren, and even the husband's three siblings, all still living in their late eighties or early nineties. Each November, the couple heads down to West Palm Beach, Florida to escape the cold winter in the North. At social gatherings, one may notice a distinct pride and self-respect that leads the man, always well-groomed in a well-pressed suit, to involuntarily rise out of his seat and stand tall to shake the hands of those who approach him, young and old alike. One might also observe the appreciation for life and love that has kept him happily married for so many years, still dancing with his wife and kissing her on the cheek with a big smile on his face.

What many will not know is the part of this man's life as seen through his eyes at a pivotal time in our nation's history, which shaped the subtle character traits that have come to define him in the present day. Wandering up to the second floor of that two-story Kings Park home, there is an indistinct room to the left, clad with black-and-white photographs of a different kind than those in the living room: memorabilia, medals, and awards from a global conflict of which there are less and less living survivors each year; pictures of friends and soldiers in their prime during training at Fort Bragg, many of whose lives ended prematurely and abruptly in a foreign land. The room reflects an experience that is so different from those of ordinary citizens, and all too similar to the experiences of veterans from wars throughout time; some who survived their wars, and some who did not; others who survived, but never really came home; and the stories of any of them that were never told.

This man's name is Anthony "Tony" Varone; member of the United States Army from January 1941 to June 1945; assigned to the 9th Infantry Division's 39th Infantry Regiment; squad sergeant at his highest rank; who survived eight campaigns in World War II across Algeria-French Morocco, Tunisia, Sicily, Normandy, Northern France, the Ardennes, the Rhineland, and Central Europe, escaping death and injury innumerable times, and saving a significant number of lives in the process.

This is his story.

CHAPTER TWO

Growing Up Fast

"To this day, I have never heard nor read anything from any of the men I led to safety that incredible night," recounted Tony. "I never knew their names other than the three men from my platoon. I hope they all lived a good and long life. I'd like to feel that I did help them make it home and enjoy a family life. I really wish there was a way for me to meet up with them again, just to make me feel it wasn't all for naught. I know my father must have been proud of me, for I'm sure he was with me every step of the way . . ."

Tony's parents were raised in economically contrasting households in the southern portion of mainland Italy. His father, Michael, was the youngest of sixteen children in a poor family from the Province of Caserta, thirty miles north of Naples. In Michael's teenage years, his family worked on a large plantation on the outskirts of Naples that grew oranges and olives, among other crops. As the family's most recent addition, Michael did not have to labor as much as his older siblings. He instead passed his days playing the guitar and hunting with his dog.

One afternoon while wandering about the grounds, Michael noticed a beautiful girl standing peacefully on the balcony of the main house. Her name was Maria, and she was the daughter of the plantation's wealthy owner. Michael sat beneath her balcony with his guitar in his hands and trusted canine at his side. A soft serenade compelled her to notice the humble, handsome worker looking up at her. The pair became acquainted and over time developed a tender affection for one another.

When Maria's father learned of the courtship, he considered a man of Michael's socioeconomic status beneath his daughter and chastised their love. As testament to her character, Maria refused to allow family differences to come between her and her companion. The couple spent many long afternoons sharing happiness together, and soon exchanged their marital vows.

An early lesson in life's fragility came during World War I, when Michael was called into service for the

Italian Army. He managed to survive combat and safely return home. On June 29, 1919, Maria gave birth to the first of their four children, Anthony, in Naples. Tony would welcome two sisters, Matilde and Clara, and a brother, Frederico, each nearly two and a half years apart, over the next seven years.

In 1922, the family emigrated to Brooklyn, New York. Tony was three years old. The long and treacherous journey across the Atlantic was an acceptable price for the pursuit of happiness, and an escape from the worsening conditions in Italy. Their birth country was in the midst of social and economic turmoil since the Great War. This instability would eventually lead to the rise of Prime Minister Benito Mussolini and his reign as head of the National Fascist Party for the next two decades. Although the extent of that narrative was not fully visible at the time, Michael and Maria knew enough to search for a better life in the United States of America.

It was during these first few years in Brooklyn that Tony began his life of escaping harm. The family's first apartment was located on 19th Street between 3rd and 4th Avenue. One night, the building suddenly caught fire while they were sleeping. The image of Tony's parents frantically carrying him and his sister out of the house wrapped in bed sheets would remain etched in his mind. They sat helplessly on the steps of a factory across the street and watched firefighters strenuously confront the blaze. Their first home in America burned to the ground over the course of the night. All of their belongings, including passports and birth certificates, were destroyed.

They attempted to reclaim their lives in the basement apartment of a building on 20th Street, but their occupancy was short-lived once Maria discovered that the apartment had rats. Tony recounted his mother's frequent plea in Italian, "Michele! Michele! I'm afraid!" as she climbed atop chairs and tables.

Shuffling around the corner to an apartment on 4th Avenue between 19th and 20th Street, the family hoped that the third time would be a charm on this square block of misfortune. While at this residence, Michael and Maria welcomed their third and fourth children into the world.

Tony was six years old and had just received a brand new pair of winter gloves. It was the mid-1920s and automobile traffic was minimal compared to modern standards. By stepping onto the rear fender of an automobile and grasping the spare tire attached to the back, mischievous children would routinely hitch rides from the cars of unsuspecting drivers.

As Tony recalled, "You hid so they didn't see you, and went until the next red light and then you got off. Then you hitched back the other way."

One day, Tony decided to try this technique on a truck instead of a car. Clutching onto a chain dangling from the truck's rear, he soon felt the vehicle moving faster than he anticipated. Frightened and unaware that leaping off would require a bit of a running start, he pounced off the truck into a tumultuous tumble upon the road.

In his words, "I just let go, and down I went!"

He slid along the ground for several yards, ripping and tearing up his clothes, including his brand new winter gloves. He had to throw most of the clothes he was wearing into the trash or else his mother would have known something had transpired.

"What happened to your gloves?" she inquired after he had covered up the evidence.

"I slipped, Mom," replied her sheepish son.

Within several months, Tony's family had moved yet again. It was just outside this new residence on 43rd Street between 3rd and 4th Avenue that Tony was struck by a yellow taxicab at the age of seven.

"I still remember it," he said. "I can see myself running out of the house and down the steps with a bottle of soda, and my sister chasing after me to grab the soda from me. Next thing I know I'm running between two parked cars and 'Pow!' – there I go with wings. All I remember is flying through the air, over the parked cars, up against the wall of our house, and down."

The taxi company's lawyer deceived Maria, who was unfamiliar with American legal parlance, and the family never received compensation for their son's injuries. Tony recounts today that even a small amount of money would have substantially helped them:

"We didn't have anything. The guy made her sign a release and I wound up in the hospital all broken up for a few weeks. I don't know how we paid the medical bill."

Bills were a recurring challenge for this new American family, but one that they met with teamwork, courage, and resilience, traits that would resonate with Tony later in life.

Maria Varone was a strong and proud woman. Her fortunate upbringing had provided her with the opportunity to become well-educated, which included her gaining proficiency in Italian, French, Latin, and English. Raising four children and caring for her family in a new and foreign land was a noble endeavor. It required strength in body and mind, as she would later be called on to persevere through life's most pressing obstacles.

As Maria tended to the household, her husband vigorously pursued the income required to support their family. In the early years, Michael sold fruit, olive oil, wine, and numbers. People would pay to play the numbers, and if they won would receive a payout. All the money would go to the local mafia and Michael would receive a percentage for what he sold. As Michael established himself, he obtained a job working on the assembly line at a furniture factory. He later became a machine operator and secured a job with a different company offering him a higher salary.

While his father was navigating the labor force, the eldest child of this poor immigrant family found America to be an unforgiving place in those initial years. Tony did not have any older siblings to guide him and needed to overcome language barriers on his own. His struggle to learn English made fitting in with other children more difficult. His first attempt at finding work was equally discouraging: He was eight years old, and began selling *The Saturday Evening Post* door-to-door for a nickel. After several weeks of hustling across town, he discovered that the man on the street for whom he was working was a con artist who disappeared without ever providing Tony's share of the profits.

Still, Tony would teach himself the power of persistence over time. He learned English and found an abundance of work. As a teenager, he shined shoes on Court Street in Brooklyn. The price of a nickel, which he made sure went directly into his pocket, offered patrons the pleasure of seeing their reflection in both shoes and a brushing down of the pant legs. His childhood occupations thereafter included: cleaning liquor bottles in a liquor store; polishing furniture in a furniture store overnight while making daytime deliveries by wagon; managing a candy store while functioning as a soda jerk; and working as a delivery boy for a grocery store and a florist on the weekends.

These small jobs became more significant as the Great Depression swept through Brooklyn. Many families in the neighborhood, including Tony's, faced harsh realities of hunger and expanding poverty. Michael and Maria's eldest child did everything he could to help his family carry on through this period.

He maintained several of his jobs during and after high school, including later serving as an apprentice to his father at the furniture factory. He also worked as an usher at several movie theaters, including the Roxy Theatre in Manhattan and the Strand and Paramount Theatres in Brooklyn, among others. He later described how theatre owners would train employees for two weeks without pay and then bring in new hires every three months so they did not have to give anyone a raise. Training would include knowing not to point with an extended arm when a customer asked for the location of the ladies room, lest you poke another passing customer's eye out. Instead, you were taught to point with your hands in front of your chest and close to your body.

In his words, "They taught you all that and you only had the job for three months at a time."

Notwithstanding the extent of his occupations, Tony managed to be an honor roll student at Brooklyn Manual Training High School located on 7th Avenue between 4th and 5th Street. Among his extracurricular activities, he served on the Traffic Squad, which required him to maintain order in the halls and navigate crowds of students safely through congested areas in-between classes.

One day, a cheerful girl came strolling down the hallway with a few friends at her side. Her name was Viola, and she was two years younger than Tony. She had taken notice of the handsome upperclassman some time before and made up her mind to finally approach him. He was wearing a small pin of a Scottish terrier on his lapel.

"What a cute dog!" Viola exclaimed brightly. "What a nice dog you got there! That's a Scotty, isn't it?"

"Yeah," Tony responded coyly as he continued directing traffic.

"Gee! Well I'm going to call you Scotty!" she said with a grand smile. Tony grinned and nodded his head, and the young girl went on her way.

Viola had regularly noticed Tony walking his sister Matilde to school in the morning. He would gentlemanly hold his sister's arm at the elbow as she stepped on and off the curb. Tillie, as she was called, was in the same grade as Viola, but the two did not know each other. One morning, Viola shyly walked over to Tillie's desk.

"Excuse me," Viola said, "The boy who walks with

you, is that your boyfriend?"

"No, that's my brother Tony," Tillie responded politely with surprise in her voice.

"Oh, okay. Well, thank you very much!" Viola said bashfully.

The two schoolgirls became close friends and as a result, Tillie and Tony's other sister, Claire, soon adopted the nickname "Scotty." Viola had an eye for their older brother, and the pair eventually went on a few friendly dates during high school, although nothing materialized at the time.

VARONE, ANTONIO—431 Bay Ridge Avenue—90% Certificate for Biology; 2 Letters of Commendation; Junior Arista 3; Bank Agent 5, 6; Secretary to Mr. Rosenberg 4, 5, 6, 7, 8; P. T. Squad Leader 1, 2, 4, 5, 6, 7; Honor Guard 4, 5, 6, 7; Traffic Squad 4, 5, 6, 7; Biology Laboratory Squad 1, 2, 4, 5, 6, 7, 8; 56 Service Credits.—Cornell.

Extract from Tony's high school senior yearbook – 1938

Tony's family continued to change apartments every few years for the financial benefits, namely that new landlords would provide one month's free rent and freshly painted walls. The children adapted to their ever-changing environment, and Michael and Maria appreciated the periodic relief in their struggle to feed, clothe, and shelter the family.

In 1938, Tony's high school record earned him acceptance onto the waiting list at Cornell University. Unfortunately, his parents could not afford to send him to college, so the senior did not pursue the opportunity further. The family now lived at 431 Bay Ridge Avenue and it was to this address, in that same year, that Tony received a letter from Benito Mussolini. Tony was still an Italian citizen and the standardized letter demanded that he report for his mandatory two-year enlistment in the Italian Army. It warned that if he did not oblige, he would never again be allowed to set foot on Italian soil, not even to visit his many relatives. If he did try to enter the country, he would be arrested and jailed.

Tony's mother took the letter from his hands gently into hers. She seemed pensive. Her lips were pursed and her eyes narrowed as if reflecting on the country she had left behind in 1922. She slowly ripped the letter in half and placed the pieces on the table in front of her. She turned to her son and softly ended her silence with four sincere words: "We are Americans now."

Two years later, in October 1940, Tony volunteered for the United States Army. The Japanese had invaded China. Germany and the Soviet Union had invaded Poland. Tensions were heightening on a global scale. Tony knew that he wanted to serve his country and to receive as much training as possible before going to war.

On January 16, 1941, he reported to Camp Upton, Long Island. He recalled lining up with his fellow recruits in the early morning hours to march for several miles in the snow. Some of them came out of the barracks in only their undergarments and an overcoat. There would be a steep learning curve to ascend in the months ahead. After a few days at Camp Upton, the green recruits packed up for Fort Bragg, North Carolina. The long journey to becoming soldiers had begun.

Tony with his brother Frederick at Camp Upton.

– January 1941 –

CHAPTER THREE

A Life in Training

Tony entered Fort Bragg at the rank of private and was assigned to Company C of the 9th Infantry Division's 39th Infantry Regiment. After several weeks of basic training, the men were issued a brief weekend of leave in February of 1941 in honor of George Washington's birthday, the holiday later known as President's Day. While the thirteen-hour bus route from North Carolina to New York left him with only a few hours to see his family, Tony managed to capture a few memories in photographs, including one notable moment with his father standing proudly beside him on the sidewalk outside their house.

Tony with his father Michael in Brooklyn. – February 1941

Basic training resumed with physical conditioning, obstacle courses, and hours of target practice firing weapons such as the Browning Automatic Rifle (B.A.R.) and 1903 Springfield. Tony described his experience in a letter to his mother dated March 11, 1941. He was twenty-one-years-old:

"*. . . Gee whiz, does the gun I have make noise. All I could hear all day was the noise of bullets. There were close to four thousand soldiers there with me and about five hundred soldiers would fire at a time . . . So far I am making expert and I hope that I don't make any mistakes the rest of this week to spoil my score. The first bullet I shot scared me and I pulled the gun back [and] scratched my nose with my thumb. It isn't anything but a scratch; so don't worry.*

I was on the firing line four times today and I think it was great . . . We are to be out on the range, which is about a mile and a half from the company street, before the sun comes up. It was still dark this morning when we got there, so we had time to smoke and sit around and talk. About a quarter to seven . . . some of them already started to fire their rifles. It started to rain real hard. We couldn't go back but had to lay there in the rain anyway and fire. It stopped about 11:30 a.m. and at noon we had lunch. The sun was really good and hot right after lunch and I sure did get a sweet sunburn. I tell you, it is a good thing it came out because the ground dried up and it wasn't so bad to lay in . . .

Mom, I think this is the best thing about the Army because it is very interesting and it sort of makes one want to get the highest score and stand out more than the other fellow . . . Wish me luck will you Mom."

A week later on March 18, Tony shared the following:

> *" . . . I had a little fun today with the other boys. We were being taught how to fall on a gun if you trip while walking through the woods or on a plain where there are lots of small holes and stumps. One boy didn't have as much fun because he didn't understand how to do it . . . he broke his nose and got seven stitches. You see he fell on his gun with his face . . . Don't worry about me making mistakes though because I catch on quick, and I won't get hurt . . . "*

Tony earned an expert badge for his proficiency with the rifle, and additional badges of recognition for his competence with the pistol, bayonet, grenade, and machine gun. He hoped such experience would help him become an effective soldier and survive combat in later years. This was the reason he had volunteered for the Army instead of waiting to be drafted.

Outside of training, soldiers were required to perform routine chores and duties around the barracks. Discipline in their speech, movement, and appearance was the foundation of their conduct. Each day a selection of soldiers was chosen to perform guard duty. Due to the high number of trainees on the premises, a given soldier was picked roughly once every twelve weeks. Guards were lined up for review by an officer and expected to present themselves in perfect uniform: unwrinkled shirts, crisp pants, shined shoes, straight laces, and their rifles in order. The soldier who best demonstrated these criteria was chosen to be the colonel's orderly for twenty-four hours of duty while the rest were dispatched to other posts. Tony was chosen for this privilege several times during his training at Fort Bragg. As an orderly, he stood guard outside the regimental commander's office and remained on call to perform minor duties for him. The role was better than other assignments: One night he was guarding a post outside in the rain and the weather conditions were so poor that he caught pneumonia and was hospitalized for a week.

Over time, the men progressed from advanced field exercises to large-scale maneuvers intended to prepare officers and soldiers alike for the experience of combat overseas. At their highest level, maneuvers encompassed hundreds of thousands of American troops across multiple divisions, complete with vehicles, weapons, and equipment, and stretched across several U.S. states. One American unit would compete against another American unit in simulated strategic battle with each side wearing red or blue ribbons on their helmets to distinguish their allegiance. Officers serving as umpires would indicate who had fallen and who had survived. Naturally, no live ammunition was fired.

Tony described one of his earliest maneuvers in a letter home dated June 21, 1941. His frequent correspondence with his parents and siblings reflected the strong connection he had with them and his desire to make them proud and assured of his well-being. He described his experiences with passion and enthusiasm, and spent many dollops of ink reiterating his love and gratitude for his family and all they had done for him throughout his upbringing. The maneuvers would expand in scope, duration, and complexity over the next several months, however the following letter exemplified their basic concept:

"Dearest Mom, Dad, and Kids:

This is your Anthony again giving you all a blow-by-blow description of what's what here and with me. But before I start, I want to tell you how happy your precious and sweet letters touched my heart. Gosh, you all sure can say the nicest things to me and you all show me that you are thinking and loving me even more than you all say you do . . .

I take it you are all in good health and coming along fine . . . Please keep it that way, for I feel happy when I know that there isn't anything wrong at home. I too feel swell and mighty healthy. It's true that I get tired at times but that is to be expected.

I believe that you all want to know about the problem I was on last Wednesday and Thursday, so here goes. Wednesday morning we got up at the usual hour for work and did the daily routine until lunchtime. After lunch we were told to prepare for the problem and be ready to move out by 1:30 p.m. At first we thought that we were going to march all the way to the designated point and back, but our thoughts were changed, for at 1:30 p.m. we saw a long, long line of trucks waiting for us to board them. And so we did. We rode for three hours or more and finally we stopped and we were told to pitch tents, for we were to remain there for the rest of the night.

At 5:30 p.m. we had dinner and right after that the regiment was called in columns of companies to have the problem explained . . . We were told that we were to fight our sister regiment, the 47th (also at Fort Bragg), which was a few miles away from the position we were occupying. You see it was going to be a battle between the two regiments and blank ammunition was going to be used. Right after the explanation we were told to go to bed but certain fellows were to take guard around the company for one hour and they were to be relieved by the next group. We all had a turn at it.

The objective, that is for the battle, was to see if the 47th Infantry Regiment could hold us from getting to Fort Bragg . . . At 4:00 a.m. we were awoken. After breakfast we were given three sandwiches of jelly and peanut butter to carry us through our lunch hour until the time came for us to have dinner . . . The Captain appointed two squads from the first platoon (I am in that platoon) and one Browning Automatic Rifle man to go with the two squads. I was the B.A.R. man that was chosen . . . It is a swell gun to handle. There is an ammunition carrier and an assistant B.A.R. man along with me at all times . . . The mission of us appointed men was to discover the position of the enemy, the number of men there were, where their strongest points were, the best way to break through them, and to send back a man with all that information to the regimental command post of our infantry regiment so that the commanding officers could build up our line and be able to work out a good method of attack . . . After sending back the information, we had to give the enemy as much trouble as possible so as to give our men time to plan the attack and place themselves.

After a bitter battle without any bloodshed we were pushed back into our own lines. We were outnumbered nine to one. The Captain admired our work even though we were forced back because our job was just as I explained, and we did all that. Naturally, when the enemy reached our lines they didn't know it until the command was given for all those in <u>our</u> front lines to fire and when we did we captured many hundreds of *them and pushed the rest so far back that the umpires gave us the battle and called it a good day's work . . . The battle was very long and close to 25,000 rounds of ammunition were fired by our [Thirty-Ninth] Infantry Regiment alone.*

The officers finally got together after the battle and they had a good talk. About a half hour later the officers of the 47th Infantry Regiment admitted defeat and said that the umpires showed them their mistakes quite efficiently. Not that they didn't know that they lost the battle before that, but the talk was more to show where their mistakes were made so that they would not make the same mistakes again. We had a great time ribbing the soldiers of the 47th for losing the battle . . ."

The men returned to Fort Bragg and life continued in this way for the next several months. Individual maneuvers lasted upwards of five days at a time. While these experiences forged physical strength, tactical knowledge, and personal discipline, they could not replicate or prepare the men for the true and hideous nature of war. Peanut butter and jelly sandwiches, blank ammunition, and weekend rest periods would soon become distant memories. Tony likely suspected as much, although he would not let on to it. On August 17, he wrote to his brother to share that he had volunteered as a lifeguard at the Fort and saved a soldier who was drowning. He was healthy, confident, and in high spirits. In the same letter, he wrote to his father that he believed the enemy would cower once they saw that the United States was prepared to enter the conflict, and there would be no war. Perhaps his words were a loving attempt to ease the concerns of his worried father. While his prediction would of course be proven false, Tony would, at least for now, focus on making the most of life in the months ahead.

In the fall of 1941, the 39th Infantry Regiment travelled to Rock Hill, South Carolina to begin an extended period of maneuvers apart from Fort Bragg. On the weekend of September 26, a friend and fellow solider named Arty inquired if Tony would like to join him on a seemingly trivial adventure. Arty was an enthusiastic gambler from Buffalo, New York who won his fair share of money playing cards and rolling dice with other soldiers. He was also a hunter, fisherman, and great outdoorsman who taught Tony valuable skills such as how to assemble and disassemble his rifle.

Aside from his more practical knowledge, Tony's comrade knew how to have fun. The boys had originally intended to go fishing on a lake not far from the company, but heavy rain from the week prior made the conditions along the river muddy and unfavorable. Arty now had bigger plans. His proposal was to take a public bus thirty miles north to the refuge of Charlotte, North Carolina for a steak dinner and night of dancing with girls from the bustling college town.

They arrived in Charlotte with excitement and anticipation for the hours ahead. These same sentiments were undoubtedly responsible for their neglecting to check the return bus schedule. After an energetic evening, they were all about ready to head back when they realized that the next bus was not leaving until the following morning, arriving hours after Company C was scheduled to begin its first maneuver from Rock Hill. The girls who they had met had access to a car and were sympathetic to the boys' plight. They offered to drive them the entire way home, but quickly realized they too needed to be back in their dorm rooms for bed checks, and could only take the young men part of the way.

Long after midnight and about ten miles short of Rock Hill, Tony and Arty bid farewell to their sprightly companions whose car turned slowly back towards Charlotte. The two boys in uniform glanced at each other with amusement and despair. They had consumed their fair share of beverages and danced the night away. Needless to say, they were in no condition for the trek before them, despite months of conditioning. They had walked along the road for several miles when they decided in a desperate reach for prudence that one of them should sleep while the other kept an eye out for someone who could offer them a lift. As one might expect such a scenario to unfold, both of them fell asleep beside each other on the side of the road. It was not until the morning that a farmer on a horse-drawn wagon found them:

"You crazy GI's!" cried the farmer. "Are you trying to get yourselves killed laying like that in the middle of the road?"

"Well, we're on the side of the road, not the middle of the road. We were hoping to get a lift."

"Alright. Hop on! I'll take you a few miles down the road."

When the young men finally returned to camp at eight-thirty in the morning, four hours after the company had set off on its first maneuver, their first sergeant was enraged:

"You went AWOL! I am going to have your ass! From now on, I'm giving you orders!"

It was at this juncture that Tony was declared absent without leave for the first of two occasions, neither of which were very accurate descriptions; he had volunteered for the Army and deserting was the last thing on his mind. A more appropriate term would have been ALWOL, or "*accidentally late* without leave." After all, they had merely failed to check the bus schedule. Nevertheless, the first sergeant put Tony and Arty on temporary house arrest and made them run a gauntlet of chores for the next several weeks.

The deviant pair was ordered to dig multiple holes in the ground with a length, width, and depth of six feet. When they finished digging a particular hole, the first sergeant would throw his cigarette inside and tell them to quickly fill it back up with dirt. They were ordered to clean toilets, serve extended kitchen duty, peel potatoes, and wash dishes, among a plethora of other tasks. All of the chores were scheduled during rests in maneuvers so they relied on very little sleep.

The final component of their sentence was having their pay reduced from thirty-dollars to twenty-one-dollars per month. Since food and shelter was provided for trainees, the Army encouraged soldiers to send money home to their families; Tony sent fifteen dollars from each paycheck. For other goods and services, soldiers would purchase books of voucher stamps for one dollar a piece. Each book would contain stamps worth five or ten cents that could be exchanged for whatever they needed. Tony paid just over one dollar per month for his laundry, and also liked to purchase cigarettes and an occasional can of beer. Having only a few dollars of discretionary spending per month did not help his morale.

After a few weeks of moving back and forth between maneuvers and chores, not to mention being ridiculed by the other men, Tony's frustration reached its peak. He wrote home to his family and friends about his unfortunate circumstances. In a turn of good fortune, he learned that a bookkeeper named Ms. Siegel, who worked in the same furniture factory as Tony and his father, had a brother in the 39th Infantry Regiment. She told the family that her brother was being assigned to a new Anti-Tank Company that was just being formed and in need of additional men. Tony made the connection with her brother and requested to speak with the commander of the Anti-Tank Company.

He portrayed to the commander how his situation had grown increasingly difficult ever since he accidentally missed the bus from Charlotte. He reiterated his commitment to the Army and his desire to work hard for the newly formed company. The hesitant leader advised Tony that this endeavor would entail much more than simply working with a rifle and a bayonet as in a normal infantry company and would instead demand the likings of a top-notch soldier. Tony would need to learn how to arm and disarm American, British, Italian, and German mines; he would have to know the weights of the mines and how to disable booby traps in complete darkness; and he would need to master the use of anti-tank guns.

Even Arty, who was inclined to follow his friend to a new company, thought Tony was ill-advised to volunteer to fight tanks with rifles, mines, and bazookas. Nevertheless, Tony said he would rather learn these skills and better himself as a soldier than remain under the relentless authority of his current first sergeant. He told the commander that he would be that top-notch soldier. His successful transfer to the Anti-Tank Company followed and he was assigned to its 3rd platoon where he hoped for a new beginning.

On the morning of Sunday, December 7, 1941, Japan attacked Pearl Harbor. By the end of the week, the United States had entered the war. The nation was both shaken and incensed. However, for a young man who had already overcome his fair share of obstacles growing up, and who was about to endure several years at war, one much more personal emotional obstacle still came before him: In the same month that thousands perished on the shores of Hawaii and the war thrust itself into the forefront of reality,

Tony's father Michael suffered a massive heart attack contemplating the fears and emotions of his son fighting and killing Italian friends and relatives overseas.

Tony was permitted a leave from Fort Bragg during which he was able to spend a few final days with his father before returning to North Carolina. On December 28, he received a telegram from his mother expressing renewed concern. On December 29, Michael died. He was forty-three years old. Tony rushed back to a grieving home where he consoled his mother and siblings.

Michael's life and death would become a source of strength for Tony throughout the war, with thoughts of his father watching over him serving as an oasis of peace and security amid the chaos.

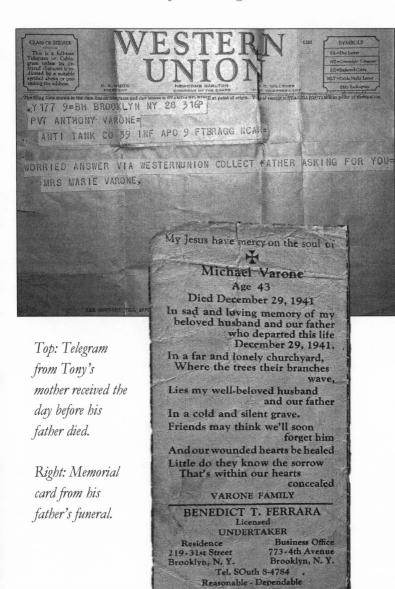

Top: Telegram from Tony's mother received the day before his father died.

Right: Memorial card from his father's funeral.

35

Private Varone in uniform at Fort Bragg with his
M1903 Springfield rifle and 1917-A1 helmet.
— 1941 —

CHAPTER FOUR

Into Unknown Seas

The wake was held inside the family's home. Looking down over his father's body with emotional wounds still forming in his heart, Private Varone wrestled with a pressing obligation to return to Fort Bragg. His emergency leave would not be long enough to enable him to attend his father's funeral and burial. It was a painful reality that he solemnly accepted. To make matters worse, he was still two days late returning to North Carolina despite his sacrifice. The Army declared him AWOL for the second time. The consequences were less severe in this instance given the circumstances. He later commented that notifying his superiors of his need for an extension would have likely pardoned him, but bereavement clouded his mind from such considerations.

Back at Fort Bragg, the Army was focused on the mobilization of its forces. The pace and tone of each day intensified in the weeks and months after Pearl Harbor. As foretold by his new commander, Tony received invaluable mine training with the Anti-Tank Company. He would later utilize this tactical and technical knowledge consistently throughout the war.

During this time, Tony also trained as a first gunner on the 37-millimeter anti-tank gun. He and the other men performed demonstrations when foreign dignitaries visited the Fort to showcase how quickly they could set up and fire the weapons at tanks and other targets. A photograph of this scene was captured during a visit from British leadership.

Tony (foreground, second from left, face obstructed)
demonstrating the 37-millimeter anti-tank gun to the British.
– 1942 –

By the spring of 1942, the men of the 9th Infantry Division transitioned to amphibious training. Ocean maneuvers were performed on large merchant ships used during peacetime to transport fruits, vegetables, and other cargo. Troops were at sea for multiple-week intervals to replicate the conditions of sailing across the North Atlantic. They practiced descending rope ladders onto smaller boats carrying all their gear, and simulated taking over beaches, ports, and U.S. marine bases along the eastern coast of the United States and in the Chesapeake Bay.

Ship conditions were grim for the American GI's. The sleeping quarters were packed tightly into the hull. Cots were stacked as many as six bunks high with hundreds of men aboard a single vessel. When soldiers on the top bunk were seasick, they would sometimes vomit off the side of the bunk onto everyone beneath them.

Rations were equally poor, consisting of canned and dried food, bread, onions, and beans. Eventually, Tony discovered that the crew of the merchant ship was eating better than its passenger GI's. When an opportunity arose to serve as a gunner for the ship, he volunteered. In accepting this role, he was relieved of the routine drills and exercises around the deck, and entitled to eat a higher quality of hot and cold meals with the merchant crew.

He was likewise assuming a true responsibility. While maneuvers were only training exercises, real dangers lurked beneath the ocean's surface. German submarines were sinking American ships headed to Europe carrying men, food, and supplies. There was nothing to distinguish training boats from those headed overseas, and the Germans would not care either way. To defend against this threat, merchant ships were equipped with various weapons carrying live ammunition. Gunners worked in shifts of four hours on and eight hours off. Tony was assigned to the 20-millimeter antiaircraft gun and later the 50-caliber. These powerful weapons were large, shielded turrets mounted onto the ship on steel pedestals. A soldier stepped into shoulder rests that allowed him to use the scope and manipulate the gun against a moving enemy target.

During a break on land in the Chesapeake Bay, Tony ran into Arty, who was still with Company C. The two men went out on the town one last time, sharing much laughter and amusement in the summer sun. They returned to their respective companies well ahead of curfew. It was their final rendezvous before heading off to war. They would not see each other again for a very long time, and the circumstances of their next meeting would be completely unlike anything that came before.

Ocean maneuvers were completed by the end of the summer, and the Ninth reassembled at Fort Bragg. In September, the soldiers of the 39th Infantry Regiment, also known as "The Fighting Falcons," were instructed to pack up their belongings and send home or discard anything displaying their name and unit, or that had the potential to reveal who they were, where they were, and to which outfit they belonged. Tony sent home his personal belongings, including a tube radio that he still has to this day. The men were sent on trains to Fort Dix, New Jersey, from where they were then transported to Staten Island on September 24. They would soon board ships headed to Europe.

On the evening of the 24th, Tony overheard that a GI ambulance was heading out on a round-trip to Fort Hamilton in Brooklyn. His widowed mother had moved the family to 5th Avenue and 51st Street following her husband's death. Their new home was only a few miles from Fort Hamilton and could easily be passed along the ambulance's route. Tony asked the ambulance driver if he could come along for the ride. The driver accepted his request and they snuck off into the night.

The Verrazano Bridge, which today connects Staten Island and Brooklyn, did not enter construction until 1959. Therefore, the ambulance had to travel through

New Jersey to the Holland Tunnel and across the Brooklyn Bridge to reach its destination. Tony said farewell to his mother and siblings in a period of less than an hour, and the GI ambulance picked him up on its return to Staten Island. He was in his bed that night without anyone ever knowing he left.

On September 25, Tony boarded the *USS Leedstown*, one of several cargo ships scheduled to set sail the next morning with members of the 39th Infantry Regiment. He was apprehensive about their chances of a safe passage. After a brief stop in Nova Scotia, the large fleet of Allied ships set out across the ocean escorted by naval battleships.

As Tony recalled, "We knew other fleets were being blown up. We had destroyers guarding our perimeter, but the nucleus was just the merchant ships transporting us. While on duty as a gunner, I would look for ripples from the submarines' periscopes and changes in the darkness of the water."

Thankfully, Tony never encountered fire from a German vessel. Still, he considered volunteering as a gunner to be a decision that helped him beat the odds in the years that followed. Aside from being afforded improved rations and sleeping quarters, he was able to familiarize himself with the experience of waiting indefinitely for an unknown enemy. Preparing mentally for combat could be daunting. Harder still was not knowing when and if there would be combat. Properly handling the psychological aspects of such uncertainty was an acquired skill that harbored a soldier's composure and decision-making facilities. Serving as a gunner thus rendered Tony in better physical and mental condition heading into the war.

After ten days crossing the North Atlantic, the Thirty-Ninth landed with the rest of its fleet in Belfast, Northern Ireland. The GI's were given a couple of weeks to recover and receive better rations after their long journey. Once restored, they sailed to Inveraray, Scotland for more ocean maneuvers on friendly foreign soil. They prepared and executed landing simulations for several days, replicating the rope ladder descents and securing of the shores that they had practiced earlier on their native coastline.

Leaving Scotland, the fleet returned to the North Atlantic to engage in a series of navigational twists and turns intended to obscure Allied plans from the enemy. By this time, Tony had switched from the *USS Leedstown* to another vessel. Sailing westward towards the States and back east towards Europe, southward towards the Strait of Gibraltar and back up towards Northern Ireland, the fleet repeatedly altered course as the troops waited for naval ships to join them for what would be their first invasion.

This period at sea lasted several days longer than expected and conditions for the GI's deteriorated as food and supplies became limited. Nevertheless, the Thirty-Ninth readied itself for action.

Operation Torch waited on the horizon.

CHAPTER FIVE

First Landing

By the closing months of 1942, British troops had been wrestling with Italian and German forces in Libya and Egypt for nearly two years. Hitler's success in Europe heightened the strategic significance of the North African region, which either side could utilize as a launching point for attacks over the Mediterranean Sea and as a medium for transporting troops and supplies. The German leader in North Africa was Field Marshall Erwin Rommel, who came to be known as the "Desert Fox" for his tactical prowess in tank warfare and aggressive maneuvering across the harsh and barren landscape.

On November 8, Allied forces consisting of American and British troops launched Operation

Torch, a three-pronged amphibious invasion of French-controlled Morocco and Algeria, targeting the coastal cities of Casablanca, Oran, and Algiers. Operation Torch was planned to quickly seize the ports and airfields of the three cities, and serve as the prelude for a rapid advancement into Tunisia to capture the German strongholds of Bizerte, the northernmost point of Africa, and Tunis, forty miles south. The Vichy French government, established by France following the country's surrender to Germany in 1940, now controlled the French colonies of Morocco and Algeria. They were Nazi-influenced and despite Allied diplomatic attempts to have French troops surrender prior to the Allied landings, resistance ensued. After three days of fighting, Operation Torch was complete.

The 39th Infantry Regiment had been part of the Eastern Task Force, which was responsible for capturing Algiers, the city nearest to the German main force. The invasion progressed in the same manner as the ocean maneuvers that they had rehearsed time and time again. Men loaded themselves onto smaller boats using ropes from the main ship as the waves swelled around them. The city fell by nightfall of the first day with limited resistance.

As Tony recalled, "The French were firing at us but it was not too horrific. They only had a few artillery pieces."

The Eastern Task Force soon captured the Maison Blanche Airport and established itself in the surrounding area. Tony recounted an amusing moment from this time that occurred while he and his fellow men were stationed near a winemaking operation. The outdoor position was adjacent to a group of tall wine vats with ladders along their sides and wooden planks across their otherwise exposed openings. One day a reclusive soldier decided to take a nap on one of the planks. He extended his legs and crossed his feet in a supine position with his hands on his chest and his helmet covering his eyes from the sun. Not long after falling asleep, his placid body rolled off the plank and flopped neck-deep into a pool of wine amid a sea of laughter from the other men. Such images would contribute themselves to the lighter memories of the war.

Alcohol indirectly played another beneficial role for Tony while in Algiers. One evening a particular corporal was found stumbling about drunk on duty and busted down to a private. Prior to his demotion, the corporal had served as the runner for Tony's platoon. Runners were depended upon in combat to physically relay orders and intelligence among platoon

leaders and the higher commands of a company.[1]
Tony had recently been promoted to corporal. Now,
as a result of his fellow soldier's insobriety, he was
also selected as the new runner for the 3rd platoon.
Although his predecessor did not leave much to be
desired, the role of runner was a meaningful
improvement for Tony, whose previous role as a first
gunner on an anti-tank gun carried less responsibility
and higher risks.

Following his promotion, Tony was ordered to help
train some of the other men. Soldiers working in the
kitchen often missed valuable combat training, so he
was directed to instruct them on how to use their
weapons and disarm enemy soldiers. One of the first
lessons he had learned in training at Fort Bragg was to
not sharpen your bayonet. A sharp bayonet could
stick into the bones of the enemy and leave you

---

[1] A brief description of how soldiers were organized is perhaps
warranted: From a structural perspective, the 39th Infantry
Regiment was organized into several battalions each containing
four companies. A company consisted of approximately two
hundred men. Each company was divided into four equally
numbered platoons, which were further divided into four
equal squads. A lieutenant and platoon sergeant commanded a
platoon while a lower-ranking sergeant and corporal were
assigned to each squad. The squad sergeant would lead a
formation in battle while his corporal brought up the rear,
prepared to replace him should he be killed or wounded. An
additional corporal who was unaffiliated with a squad served as
the sole runner for the platoon and reported directly to the
lieutenant in command. Such was in part the manner in which
thousands of men united on the battlefield.

vulnerable to another attacking combatant. He relayed this lesson to the men from the kitchen, but a cook who clearly liked to sharpen everything, sharpened his bayonet all the same. Later on, Tony regrettably selected to demonstrate on the cook how to flip an enemy soldier on his back by grabbing his weapon and throwing him over your leg. Tony grabbed the cook's gun at the presumably dull bayonet and slit three fingers right across the palm of his hand. Friendly fire.

Over time, more and more supplies came into the harbor at Algiers. The men formed stockpiles along the road, which the Germans bombarded with aircraft whenever possible. At this early stage in the campaign, the Americans had not secured enough territory to enable planes of their own to land. Restrained by how far their fuel tanks could carry them, American fighter planes were unable to provide sufficient support to the men on the ground. Defense was thus limited to artillery and antiaircraft weapons until a greater perimeter could be established.

Three months after landing in North Africa, Tony's circumstances remained tolerable. There had been air raids and minor skirmishes on the ground. He had endured nights without sleep and hours of patrol and reconnaissance across hostile foreign land. Yet, he remained unharmed and untested by an enemy that seemed to be somewhere off in the distance. A series of letters to his siblings dated January 15, 1943 portrayed optimism coupled with a sincere and salient nostalgia for home and country. Several months had passed since their last correspondence:

North Africa
January 15, 1943

My Dear Tillie,

Here I am once again after a very long time writing and letting you know that I am in the best of health and feeling fine. I guess I'll always feel that way for I know that's the only way to feel and stay if I ever want to get back home safe and sound. So please don't worry about me . . .

~~~

Dear Freddie,

How are you? According to your letter of November 11, which I received the other day with Tillie's, I gather that this world of ours is treating you fine. I really am glad to learn that for knowing that you are having a good time makes me feel tops and makes me want to fight twice as hard to keep you that way. Nobody will ever take away from you or anybody else in the United States the freedoms we have. We earned them and we are going to fight hard to keep them always . . .

By the way, how do you like high school? Are you going out for any teams? Did you play any big games? Tell me all about it and everything else next time you write . . . Don't worry about me, and help take care of everything until I get back home! Good luck and lots of love . . .

~~~

My Dear Clara,

I do hope you received all my letters for I wrote at least 18 of them if not more. I also wrote a few postal cards before I got to my first destination . . .Give Mom a big birthday kiss for me and tell her I love her more than anyone in the whole world. Love and kisses to you.

Your loving brother,

Tony

In early February, the Anti-Tank Company was dispatched on small trucks to secure a German airfield in the city of Biskra, an oasis along the upper edge of the Sahara Desert over two hundred and fifty miles southeast of Algiers. The men reached their destination and remained on quiet guard duty for a couple of weeks awaiting British Spitfire planes to land and refuel. Unbeknownst to Corporal Varone, the lighter chapter of the war that he had experienced up until this point was drawing to an abrupt conclusion, with no period ahead holding its slightest resemblance.

A sudden emergency call from headquarters instructed all available units to report immediately to Kasserine Pass, the site of a narrow one-mile opening along a mountain chain in central Tunisia. The Desert Fox had launched a commanding offensive up from southern Tunisia intended to reach Tebessa, an Allied stronghold along the Algeria-Tunisian border housing large quantities of fuel and supplies. The Allies were losing ground and suffering severe casualties with inferior weapons and inexperienced men. Given its forward position at Biskra, the Anti-Tank Company was ordered ahead of the Ninth to aid in the establishment of defensive lines that would hinder the enemy and provide cover for Allied troops struggling to escape.

Two hundred hearts and minds hastily loaded onto trucks and travelled farther in miles than in men, through Tebessa, to the town twenty-five miles north of Kasserine Pass known as Thala. By this point,

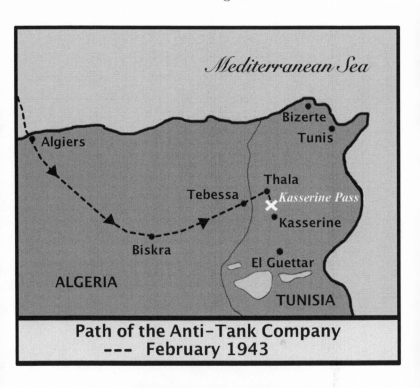

Path of the Anti-Tank Company
--- February 1943

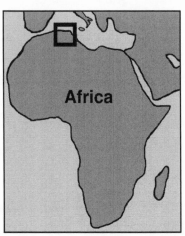

Rommel's powerful German tanks had mercilessly decimated the 1st Armored Division among other Allied units. Driving south along the road between Thala and Kasserine, the Anti-Tank Company's convoy was suddenly forced onto the shoulder. The path needed to be cleared for traffic coming from the opposite direction.

Tony stared ahead in disbelief as his eyes processed an image that would be forever etched in his mind: Thousands of wounded, bewildered, exhausted, and terrified American soldiers slowly weaved up the road from the direction the Anti-Tank Company was headed. Trucks and jeeps containing stretchers were overwhelmed with injured personnel. The infantrymen who could walk did so on either side of the road by the hundreds. Some had bandages on their heads; others had their arms in slings. Their faces looked tired and devastated. They were dirty, dusty, and unshaven. Even tanks rolled along in retreat to escape the slaughter, many of them severely damaged in accordance with the men at their helms.

Time was nearing the weekend of Washington's Birthday, February 1943. Two years ago, Tony had been on holiday leave with his family, posing with his father for the photograph in front of their house. Twelve months later, he had been training with the Anti-Tank Company at Fort Bragg with the grief of his father's recent passing still fresh in his mind. Now the present moment seemed a lifetime apart from such memories.

In his words, "My stomach flipped and my heart started to beat loud enough for my family back home to hear it. Chills ran up and down my spine and I prayed real hard. I thought to myself, 'How can the two hundred men of my company be expected to stop this onslaught when thousands are moving back away from the fighting?' As we moved forward, we heard the men leaving yell, 'Good luck and God help you all!' They shouted as if a ferocious lion was racing towards us that could not be stopped. The German Afrika Korps were highly trained with superior combat experience and superior equipment. And here they outnumbered us. I was truly frightened to death."

Most soldiers have a moment in combat when fear overwhelms them; a moment that they can remember so vividly it is as if it happened yesterday. If they manage to survive and even persevere courageously in the face of that fear, the dangers and difficulties of war encountered after that moment carry less significance and seem to somehow process easier in the mind no matter how dreadful. The series of events that came next at Kasserine Pass was that very moment for Tony; and persevere he did.

CHAPTER SIX

I Must Return To My Men

As the dismal formation of wounded troops blended into the northern skyline, an ominous path opened up for the vehicles of the Anti-Tank Company to resume their journey to Kasserine Pass. "I'll never know what made us continue our forward movement," Tony recalled, "but forward we kept moving, onward and onward, closer and closer to the war machine that stopped at nothing; the monster that would destroy most of us as it did the men before us. The Germans watched us all from the high ground ahead. They watched not only those who were just about destroyed already, but our fresh faces of a few hundred green and untried troops against this powerful war machine before us. They must have been laughing at us with every step forward we took, just as a spider watches and waits for some unsuspecting insect to fall into its web. Closer and closer we moved towards our hell. Soon there were no other tanks, trucks, or infantrymen moving back. We were almost in Rommel's trap, and we didn't even know it."

When the company was within two miles of the pass, its commander ordered the men to set up a command post.[2] The 1st and 4th platoons would remain with the CP as a protective force while the 2nd and 3rd platoons established a defensive position one mile ahead. Riding forward with the 3rd platoon, Tony could hear the unsettling sound of explosions in the distance. His ensuing thoughts were overtaken by the commands of officers as the convoy stopped several hundred yards before a ridge leading into the combat zone. The 2nd platoon was ordered to set up on the right side of the road and the 3rd platoon on the left. Mountains rested to the northeast and southwest of their position. The platoons assembled their 37-millimeter anti-tank guns facing southeast and dug in as they were told.

Night fell and lower temperatures followed. A mysterious and harrowing calm would dance with

---

[2] A command post (CP) was a central base from which senior officers dispatched instructions to troops on the front lines up ahead. It also contained the kitchen that prepared food for the troops, and storage for their equipment and belongings.

intermittent violence to consume the long hours until dawn. Tony was cold and scared. Somewhere in the darkness, German soldiers were restoring their forces and reassessing objectives following their rapid advance from southern Tunisia. The punishing 88-millimeter artillery cannons fired less frequently in the distance, but machine guns and small arms fire could still be heard in the southeastern hills. Dispersed rounds of mortar fire rang out and planes dropped bombs attempting to kill or demoralize the remaining Allied troops on the ground.

The soldiers of the 3rd platoon were seated at the edge of no man's land without any information regarding the location and strength of enemy and friendly positions in their vicinity. There were neither radios nor telephones in these early stages of the conflict, and the enemy seemed to be jamming wireless walkie-talkie channels, which were the platoon's only other means of communication. Unable to reach its command post, the platoon anxiously guarded its position through the sleepless night.

The next morning, a jeep came barreling down the road from the north. The Anti-Tank Company's executive officer, whose role was to report directly to the company commander, was in the passenger seat. He appeared to be on reconnaissance from the command post, yet oddly never paused to check on the status of the 2nd and 3rd platoons. Instead, his jeep continued rapidly towards and over the high ground several hundred yards ahead. Before the cloud of dust from the wheels of the vehicle could settle upon the ground, a sudden barrage of assorted enemy gunfire filled the air from the other side of the ridge. Bitter silence followed and the lone jeep did not return.

By the afternoon, Tony's platoon lieutenant ordered a three-man patrol to gather intelligence. The men carefully moved ahead as the other soldiers wished them luck. Several minutes passed before a similar eruption of gunfire engulfed the patrol as it surmounted the ridge. These men, too, met an untimely end.

After one more sleepless night of fear and uncertainty, the morning brought a measure of solace. British artillery units could be seen setting up and firing calibrating rounds from a position northeast of the 2nd and 3rd platoons. Tony was relieved to learn that he and his fellow men were no longer alone. He nervously smoked a few cigarettes and engaged in meaningless banter hoping for better news in the coming hours. Beans, hash, hard crackers, chocolate bars, and a canteen of water comprised the full extent of his rations across these days and nights.

After a few hours, heavy enemy artillery shells began to fly overhead, falling deep to the rear of the 2nd and 3rd platoon. Planes strafed the ground and dropped more bombs. The platoon lieutenant turned to his runner, Corporal Tony Varone, and ordered him to determine where the Germans were positioned and any information confirming the fate of the missing men.

"It was my turn now to see the face of the enemy," said Tony in recollection. "I started out reluctantly and scared as hell. I locked and loaded my rifle; checked my four grenades, my two bandoliers of ammo, and my rifle belt. My canteen of water was half full."

He decided to move fifteen or twenty yards to the side of the road so as not to follow the same path as the unfortunate men who went before him. After walking for several minutes, he heard a rumbling from the rear. A column of six light tanks led by a British officer standing atop another tracked-vehicle called a Bren Gun Carrier was approaching his position. The officer raised his hand and the column halted alongside the road. He motioned over to Tony. The ridge was now only about two hundred yards ahead.

"Yank, what is the condition up ahead?" shouted the officer.

Tony explained his company's plight and his orders. He told the officer that he could hear firing to the left and in front of them, but did not know how many Allied troops remained. He expected that any lingering troops were scattered and abandoned, the remnants of those who had not withdrawn earlier. The officer said he intended to reconnoiter the area himself. He wanted to move his armored column to the front so that he could support any friendly troops who might still be there. Before the officer departed, Tony requested to board the Bren Gun Carrier in order to expedite his mission. He assumed a position lying on his stomach atop a flat metal plate covering the motor towards the rear of the vehicle. A gunman stood beside him manning the Bren machine gun.

As the vehicle approached the ridge, Tony realized that the heat from the motor combined with the beating sun was causing the metal plate to scorch his skin. He alerted the driver and dismounted the vehicle to travel the remaining distance on foot. He once again moved about fifteen or twenty yards to the left of the road. These small details of body placement and surface temperature over the past several minutes proved to be life saving. As the third tank following the officer's carrier breached the high point of the ridge, the enemy unloaded on the position.

Tony can still remember "the deep *belching* of the mortars, the bone-chilling *rat-tat-tats* of the machine guns, the *boom-booms* of the many big guns, the even-toned *hissing* of the small arms fire flying past." It came at the British vehicles as heavy and steady as rain and continued until the officer turned the column around and moved to the rear. At least two of the light tanks were destroyed and the officer on the Bren Gun Carrier was wounded. The gunman who had been directly next to Tony moments ago was killed along with some of his other comrades. The man's body was blue and dark from the explosion that had claimed his life.

"I was fortunate to have not gone along with them," Tony solemnly recounted. "Still I moved forward on foot towards the ridge and as I raised my head I heard a sniper round fly past my head. I rolled to my left a few feet and again I heard a shot ring out and again the shot missed me. I moved further to the right as the shooting continued in my direction."

The Germans continued to heavily bombard the area suspecting that there were more Allied troops and armored vehicles hiding on Tony's side of the ridge. He could see enemy blasts originating from the mountains along the southwestern side of the pass, and began to sprint for cover in the opposite direction. One German combatant fired a single mortar shell to calibrate his aim. It just missed Tony, who ceased in his tracks sighting the explosion in front of him. At least ten more rounds followed in rapid succession. Tony quickly turned into the direction of the distant shooter, and charged back towards the road as the raining shells continued to crash and tumble onto the ground now behind him. The lethal shrapnel from the mortars sprayed violently in the opposite direction of his movement, leaving him unscathed. Minute physical details once again proved to determine the difference between his life and death.

In his words, "To this day I'll never know how I was still alive when it all let up. It had to be my mother's prayers that saw me through that afternoon. It was as if I was in an impregnable sphere. I kept dodging the rain of mortars and artillery shelling and made it back to the road where I immediately spotted a culvert. I dashed into it and waited for the firing to end."

After nearly thirty minutes, the ground settled and a momentary calm emerged. Tony hustled back to his platoon. He told his lieutenant what happened and that there was no one to be found; he could barely surmount the ridge. He offered to try again after sundown when he would not be as vulnerable. The lieutenant told Tony he was fortunate to have survived. The platoon had still not made contact with the command post and its situation was rapidly deteriorating.

Enemy artillery fire soon reignited around the perimeter of the 3rd platoon. This latest eruption put everything Tony had experienced up until this point to shame. The 2nd platoon to the right and the British position to the rear were forced to withdraw.

"I could see flashes of weapons raining death and destruction in a pattern starting from the ridge and moving toward our position and across the road from us where there now weren't any troops at all. The shelling continued all the same covering every inch."

The entire position would soon be overrun. Tony's flustered lieutenant continued his futile attempts to contact the command post. He then turned once more to his runner, "Varone, we need help. I want you to get to the CP and ask the commander to send reinforcements [3] immediately to help us hold our position."

Perhaps this would have been a better idea earlier on. Nevertheless, Tony ran as fast as he could to relay the

---

[3] He was referring to the 1st and 4th "reserve" platoons of the Anti-Tank Company, which were still at the command post.

message. When he reached the command post a mile back up the road, he discovered that this area had also been heavily attacked by German artillery, killing and wounding some of the men. Enemy shells destroyed the kitchen and killed the cook who had accidentally injured Tony's hand with his sharpened bayonet in Algiers; he was the father of five children back home.

The unharmed soldiers worked on high alert to load food, supplies, and equipment onto trucks. The command post was evidently being moved closer towards Thala in order to safely escape German range.[4] It seemed everyone was being ordered back except for the 3rd platoon. Tony needed to find his company commander.[5]

---

[4] A common tactic for both sides in this type of warfare was to set up their long-range artillery weapons several miles behind the front lines. In this case, German observation officers atop the mountains on both sides of the pass were able to see as far north as the Anti-Tank Company's command post with their field glasses. They wired back to their artillerymen to fire for location. When they saw where the shells landed, they were able to radio in commands and adjust accordingly; such were the benefits of functioning, unscrambled communication systems. Sometimes one side's artillery cannons could reach as far back as the opposing artillery cannons. When they could not, aircraft would be sent to combat the cannons instead; and so it would continue.

[5] Command of the Anti-Tank Company had changed hands since Tony's transfer from Company C at Fort Bragg. Still, Tony knew this current commander well. They had shared time in Company C and interacted on several occasions while the commander held lower ranking positions. Once they landed in North Africa, however, Tony rarely saw him. He never came to the front lines nor addressed the soldiers individually.

When Tony delivered his message, the commander told him that the 3rd platoon must meet the onslaught outright and hold at all costs. They could not be saved and there would be no reinforcements until the command post was moved to safety. The commander likely sought to save as many men as possible for the next battle rather than sacrifice more in a futile resistance. He ordered Tony to help load the trucks and accompany them to their new command post.

Tony reluctantly obeyed. His company commander stepped into a jeep at the front of the line that would lead the troops up the road, and Tony packed into one of the open-bed passenger trucks towards the rear.

The next several minutes overwhelmed him with thoughts and emotions that made time stand still. A decision to disobey orders and return to his men would likely result in the ending of his life. His regret if he left them behind might be worse. The convoy began to roll out.

They passed a military police outpost after riding a few hundred yards. A soldier kneeling behind a large boulder was motioning troops to the rear. As Tony explained, "I saw us moving towards Thala and thought to myself, 'Wait a minute! I can't leave my guys down there. They need help and we can't send anybody else down there? They have to fight at all costs? Well, then I'm going to go die with them' . . . So I jumped off the truck."

When Tony was just a six-year-old boy in Brooklyn, he jumped from the rear of a speeding truck after holding onto its dangling chain with his brand new pair of gloves. He did so fearful of ensuing danger. Seventeen years later, he jumped from the rear of a truck in Tunisia into the heart of danger. While he fell and scraped his clothing as a child, in this defining moment he landed with firm footing.

He watched the procession of vehicles fade north into the relatively safer distance and then turned to face the now too familiar road south to Kasserine Pass. Over an hour had passed since he first left the 3rd platoon at the ridge. He walked to the MP outpost and from there watched the onslaught in the south. The sky was growing increasingly dark, yet burning vehicles and equipment provided enough light to take in the scene. White tracer bullets pierced through the clouds in the distance. Tony looked on as he gathered his bearings and mapped out a path in his mind back to the 3rd platoon. As he started out, one of the soldiers from the MP outpost confronted him.

"Are you crazy?" cried the MP. "Can't you see what's

happening down there? I have orders to send everyone towards Thala to regroup."

"Down there" was an enemy attack in full force with two other prongs making a whole lot of noise about a mile to the right and a mile to the left of the hill. Tony explained that he would not be able to live with himself if he did not go back. Eventually, the soldier capitulated: "Go ahead and get your ass shot off."

Tony fixed his bayonet to his 1903 Springfield rifle.[6] Machine gun fire from German tanks and 88's whizzing by overhead and to the rear were now the only lights in the sky. Onward Tony continued and darker the night became across the long unsettling mile. Several hundred yards northwest of the 2nd platoon's former position, Tony could hear the sound of voices. He lowered himself to a crouched position. As he crawled closer, the conversations grew louder and he realized he was in trouble for they were the voices of enemy troops.

"I started towards them thinking that it could not be so," recalled Tony, "and that somewhere along the way I had to contact friendly troops, men from any platoon, before I ran into the enemy. How wrong I

---

[6] The 1903 Springfield was a bolt-action rifle with a five-round magazine. This meant that a soldier could only fire a single round at a time and had to completely reload his weapon every five rounds.

was, for it was the enemy and no one but the enemy."

He huddled into a prickly bed of cactus plants and focused all of his attention to his ears. His eyes widened in fear and disbelief. As he stood up to move forward, he accidentally brushed some stones with his boots making a noise. German machine guns immediately unloaded a barrage in his direction.

He fell flat to the ground as he had been taught at Fort Bragg and stopped breathing. They continued to fire and move closer to him. He fired one clip of five rounds from his rifle and moved to his left. They immediately sent return fire revealing their location, and he reached for his grenades.

In his words, "I readied a grenade, pulled the pin, and waited. I became worried, so I readied a second grenade without pulling the pin. I felt I knew exactly where they were in relation to me. So I took a chance and threw my first grenade, pulled the pin on the second grenade and threw it almost into the same spot. I heard loud screams from the enemy, and threw a third and final grenade . . . I kept the last grenade for myself. If I couldn't get away, I would have rather taken some of them with me [to death] than be captured."

He made the three grenades soar high above the

enemy's position so the exploding shrapnel would rain down and cover a larger area. Thankfully, he did not need the fourth. The immediate threat had been neutralized. Still, rapid fire from tank machine guns and flares lit up the area like daylight.

"I believe they thought I was a patrol of more than one man," said Tony, "because I fired my rifle from several positions and kept moving from right to left and left to right, which was confusing in the darkness; I had been taught the move during my training with Company C. I made sure to get out of there as quickly as I could. The Good Lord was on my side for never in my life did I move so silently."

He stealthily worked his way eastward past several cactus patches and across the road to a point just north of the 3rd platoon's position. He could see his platoon lieutenant's jeep and the gun carriers burning in the distance. Enemy silhouettes milled around in the shadows of the flames and smoke. He continued towards the mountains along the northeastern border of their position to avoid detection.

Suddenly, he came upon a drop in the ground. It was a dried up riverbed, known as a wadi, common in the desert region. Under the light of the crescent moon, he observed that the wadi was shallow enough to enter and utilize as cover. He slid down into it and moved southeast along its edge.

"It was as if God had once again put me into a sphere of safety," recounted Tony.

As he approached his platoon's position from this concealed vantage point, he could see and hear more German soldiers shouting and laughing as they went through his comrades' abandoned belongings. Tony passed the preoccupied troops and witnessed firsthand the damage they had done. He confirmed that the position had been overrun; he was too late. Knowing that he could not engage the enemy alone, he searched for survivors in the moonlight.

Traveling along the wadi, Tony suddenly noticed the shadow of a man hugging the wall. He could not see much more than a few feet ahead. He pointed his rifle at the figure in the darkness prepared for the worst.

"Who's there?" Tony exclaimed.

The drained voice of a private from Tony's platoon cried out his name, rank, and serial number in a soft whisper. He no longer had his weapon.

Repeating the soldier's name with enthusiasm and disbelief, Tony responded, "Private! This is Tony Varone, Corporal Tony Varone!"

The disheartened soldier expelled an immense sigh of relief. Then he paused. "I thought everyone was dead. What happened?"

"You guys were overrun and the company commander didn't want to send men down to support or relieve you. He said you have to fight until you were killed or captured. So I'm trying to find whoever's left and bring you back to our lines. Are you alone?"

The private's eyes widened with an expression of hope. He pointed further down the wadi. "No, there are more guys down there!"

As the German advance became inevitable, the majority of Allied troops, including members of the 3rd platoon, had escaped eastward down the wadi and into the mountains. The remainder, either from exhaustion or panic, ditched their weapons and remained inside the wadi. Although seemingly counterintuitive, their reaction was a final survival tactic, counting on the hopes that a defenseless soldier would more likely be captured and taken prisoner than shot and killed.

Tony instructed the private to remain hidden, and went off to find the other men. He moved carefully along the wadi and quickly spotted another unarmed private and sergeant from the 3rd platoon. He told them to remain in place as he had told the initial private moments ago, and continued to search for more. All told, Tony discovered over a dozen scattered and abandoned troops from various companies and divisions.

As he later recalled, "I gathered all of the men together and told them how I reached them from over a mile back and that I could possibly get them all back safely if they moved behind me as silently as possible. In truth, we were surrounded and it seemed hopeless. I tried to keep my heart from beating too loud for fear the beating would give us away to the enemy. Most of those I grouped together were unarmed so a skirmish would not have been a wise move. I only wanted to get us back to our lines to fight another day when the odds would be better."

He led the chain of assorted soldiers as they trekked cautiously out of the wadi and to an outpost several miles north, between the former and newly established CPs. Guards demanded that Tony identify himself and provide a password. He told them he did not have a password because nobody gave him one. Communications were still down and there was no way for him of all people to know. He provided his name and serial number and declared fervently that he was with American GI's who had been through hell and needed some help. The guards let the men through and informed them that various jeeps were waiting a few hundred yards up ahead to transport isolated troops back to their units. When they reached the rendezvous point, the men he found from the other units parted ways in route to their respective companies. Tony knew he would never see many of them again.

"To this day, I have never heard nor read anything from any of the men I led to safety that incredible night," recounted Tony. "I never knew their names other than the three men from my platoon. I hope they all lived a good and long life. I'd like to feel that I did help them make it home and enjoy a family life. I really wish there was a way for me to meet up with them again just to make me feel it wasn't all for naught. I know my father must have been proud of me for I'm sure he was with me every step of the way."

Tony and the three men from the 3rd platoon located the 2nd platoon's lieutenant among those waiting for survivors and loaded up with him. They reached the command post a few hours before daybreak, and were given something to eat and sleeping quarters for a couple of hours of well needed rest. At dawn, the three men that Tony rescued from his platoon told their company commander the story from the previous night.

"They praised me for my heroic effort," Tony recalled. "We were all so happy to have escaped the horrible situation and still be alive."

The three men were ordered to retrieve new weapons. Tony still had his rifle and sufficient ammo. He only needed three hand grenades to replace those he had used. As he parted from the men, the second of the two privates he rescued from his platoon said to him, "You know, you're going to get the big medal for that," referring to the Medal of Honor.

Tony made light of his actions, considering them to be expected of any soldier in his position. Calm was instilled in him for the first time in several days. The worst seemed to be over.

Later that morning, a messenger summoned him to report to the company commander. Tony did not think much of it and did as he was told. He would soon learn that the calm he was experiencing resided within the eye of a larger storm.

Kasserine Pass had not yet released Tony from its grasp.

CHAPTER SEVEN

Once More into the Chasm of Death

After fleeing eastward into the mountains in escape of the German bombardment, the remainder of the 3rd platoon, including its lieutenant, were scattered and separated amid difficult, unfriendly terrain, many miles from Tony and the Anti-Tank Company's new command post. The platoon would be unable to rendezvous with the company for nearly ten days. Tony reported to his commander as requested, and was promptly reassigned to the 4th platoon. The soldiers of the 4th platoon specialized in intelligence and reconnaissance, as well as the laying down and removal of mines. They had remained with the company command post as a protective force and had not yet seen combat at Kasserine Pass. The commander expressed that he was proud of Tony's daring decision to rescue his fellow troops the previous night. Then without further thought, the commander handed him new orders. They were to be carried out immediately.

As Tony recounted, "He told me to gather the men of the mine platoon and any other men I could find and lead them down the road toward the pass to set up and defend a minefield that would delay the enemy wherever I thought best. I ordered two 2½-ton trucks and gathered about fifty men and a few hundred mines. We moved out to do whatever we could to be successful."

Tony had barely slept over the past several days. For the third time, he was heading straight into the German deathtrap while the majority of his fellow troops were compelled to retreat. He was a mere corporal, and now due to a lack of men and resources, his commander had him temporarily leading a platoon. The endeavor sounded like a suicide mission, but he understood its importance. Laying a minefield in front of the enemy's new lines would help hinder its northern advancement and provide the Allies with desperately needed time to reestablish their own lines of defense and assemble reinforcements.

As the two trucks rode towards the enemy, Tony

noticed a slight U-shaped depression to the right of the road between the higher ground behind them and comparatively lower ground ahead. The feature ran along the east-west axis and would provide decent cover against enemy fire from the south. He signaled for the drivers to stop the trucks while he inspected the area. After weighing the alternatives, Tony and the other soldiers agreed to have the 4th platoon and its supporting troops make their stand at this location.

Fifty men placed four hundred tank mines ahead of the depression in four rows parallel to their position. They set themselves up within the depression, peering south over the minefield and towards the enemy. The two trucks were parked just inside and parallel to the road now a considerable distance to their left. Scanning the area for existing mines and abandoned weapons, Tony found a British two-pounder anti-tank gun in working condition. Using knowledge from his training as a 37-millimeter anti-tank gunner at Fort Bragg, he examined the British weapon and its ammunition. Once satisfied that the gun would function properly, he instructed two fellow soldiers with anti-tank training to operate it when the time came.

Everything appeared to be in order. As the men settled into position preparing for a German attack, Tony wrestled with the peculiarity of their situation.

They had laid mines over a considerable amount of time while in full view of the enemy. He had expected the Germans to attempt to destroy the minefield and everyone within range. Instead, the Germans fired heavy artillery high over the platoon's position at Allied targets in the far north.

In his words, "I saw enemy tanks, trucks, men, and artillery in the distance. Our little group had guts or was too foolish to know any better. Hold we did, and alone at that, but I'm sure the enemy must have thought we were a million men strong. Why else would we be so fearless as to stand up and walk around our position in daylight and plain sight? I believe we made them hesitate, and perhaps become a little worried about how strong we possibly were."

Tony and his fellow troops grew restless and weary as the last hues of sunlight tucked themselves beneath the horizon. The enemy would come suddenly and shrewdly under the cover of darkness.

"We could hear the tanks rumbling toward us," he recounted. "Voices were shouting and this time I felt it was going to be the end for all of us."

One of the platoon's 2½-ton trucks was struck first. A distant tank round briskly set the truck ablaze as the platoon hit the ground for cover. Some of the men had dug foxholes earlier in the day, but most of them had been too fatigued and instead shielded themselves behind large rocks and boulders. As the flames from the exploded truck lit up the night sky, Tony gathered the men. He was the only soldier among them who had experienced close-range combat up until this point. He told them how he had managed to escape the enemy the night before and that he would lead them through the onslaught tonight, if it came to that.

Unidentified infantrymen began approaching the two trucks from the opposite side of the platoon's position. Tony could see the silhouettes of soldiers loading into the second 2½-ton truck that was still intact. The vehicles were parked too far away for him to be certain whether the men were Allied or German troops. He told his soldiers manning the two-pounder to take aim at the truck. They were to fire on his command.

The unidentified soldiers started the ignition. Tony and his men braced themselves in shooting positions with their hands on their weapons. The truck slowly began to turn towards Kasserine, and Tony could now discern German helmets in the brightness of the flames from the other truck.

In his words, "I told the men to let the enemy have it and make every shot count. We started to fire our 1903 rifles, which were once again no match for the German automatic weapons. Then our boys on the two-pounder followed through with a direct hit on the truck and enemy screams filled the air."

As the second truck exploded, killing and wounding some of the enemy, many more German infantrymen charged the platoon's position. In the lead up to the attack, Tony had been preoccupied with the organizing and directing of the men, and never had time to dig himself a foxhole. With heavy firing in both directions, he dashed across the position to establish better cover. As he hurled himself to safety behind a small boulder, a shot meant for him simultaneously struck the boulder's solid stone façade and ricocheted into the ground. Tony would have been killed in that very spot had he not fallen behind this rock.

"It was a white tracer bullet," he said. "I'll never forget it. I was a lucky guy one more time."

The enemy continued to fire and Tony desperately hurled two grenades into their midst. He could tell the enemy was shaken but was unsure of what would happen next. Suddenly, a German soldier came running towards Tony. The soldier was outside the range of the trucks' flames and in darkness. He was yelling violently what sounded like the German words for "I surrender," but he had something gripped tightly in his hand. To this day, Tony does not know whether it was a grenade or not, but he made the decision to protect himself and the men around him who would have surely been killed had an explosion occurred from that location. There was no other choice.

Eventually the Germans withdrew their attack and began heading back to their lines. It was nearly 2:00 a.m. and Tony checked on his group, which had sustained casualties. About thirty minutes later, he heard British voices approaching from behind him and shouted for them to halt. Two British officers stood before him on the higher ground. One of them asked who was in charge.

"I am," Tony responded for the first time in his military career.

"That sounded like a whole army firing away at the enemy," exclaimed the other officer.

Tony explained how the small depression echoed the thunderous sounds of the battle.

"Well. You did a great job," said the officer. "You will

be rewarded for it."

The officers then inquired if Tony and his men could hold their position until first light, when an Allied counterattack was expected to launch. Tony confirmed that his men would hold and pointed out the minefield in front of the position so that no friendly troops would be harmed.

"I had only about thirty men left and I prayed to God to hurry up the dawn," recalled Tony.

At sunrise, waves of Allied artillery hammered away at the enemy. Tony led the platoon to the right and clear of any Allied forces behind them. They went over a set of railroad tracks and then north along the tracks. Before reaching the command post, a single Messerschmitt German fighter plane flew over them strafing the ground. They ran for cover and luckily the plane went on its way. They decided to hole up in a shack alongside the tracks so as not to be attacked again. They remained there for a few hours and later continued to the rear and back behind Allied lines. When they returned to the command post, some of the other men expected Tony to receive a battlefield commission and medal for the ordeal. He was instead reequipped with more ammunition and reminded that he would soon return to combat.

Tony believed that after the war, the British were credited with the stand made by his fifty men. His company commander disappeared that same night and never reported their actions. They found the commander's jacket later on the side of the road and he was never seen again, presumed to have gone AWOL. Some of the randomly assembled men attached to the 4th platoon also disappeared during the night. Tony suspected that these men could not endure any more of the fighting and had reached a breaking point. Nevertheless, no accolades were ever mentioned about the 4th platoon's suicide mission and the considerable role they played.

"I felt good about what I was able to accomplish with so few men," said Tony. "I really and truly believe those few days were the turning point of the war in Africa against Rommel. I sometimes wonder, 'Would Rommel have reached Thala and pushed the Allied Forces back into Algeria if we didn't trick his attacking troops that night?' I suppose only God knows. Although I do hope that our courage and sacrifice over those few days did help to sustain and defend our nation's existence. There must have been many such acts throughout the war and because there weren't any newspapermen or such persons to bear witness, the deeds have gone untold. Our deeds remain in our minds, however, flashing back from time to time. Certain specifics may have dropped from my memory, but I can still remember most of what happened in those pressing days before victory was ours."

The road ahead of the Anti-Tank Company in North Africa would be long and treacherous. However, Kasserine Pass and the subsequent defense of Thala was Tony's watershed moment. He became hardened and more accepting of the fact that he could not control his fate and simply had to do the best he could to survive. He also found solace in the thought that someone must be guarding over him. He cherished his faith in God, his mother's prayers, and his departed father's guiding spirit.

In his words, "Sometimes I said to myself, 'My father's up there looking out for me. I must be walking under an impenetrable shield of glass."

Although Tony was managing to cope with his present circumstances in the war, he struggled to reconcile that experience with a notable part of his past. Before he left for the war, Tony had a girlfriend named Muriel. They dated for several years in Brooklyn before Tony volunteered for the Army and she wrote to him four or five times a week while he was at Fort Bragg. She became an extension of his family and the couple remained together heading into the war. The tube radio that he sent home before leaving the States had in fact been a gift from her. After the ordeal in Tunisia, however, Tony sent Muriel a letter that said, "After being here, and seeing what I saw, you better forget about me and make a life for yourself."

"I felt so bad that I sent it," recalled Tony, "but I did not want her to suffer for the length of the war. 'Is he going to come back? Is he not going to come back?' So I said 'Make a life for yourself,' and that's it. I sent all of her letters to my sisters to give back to her . . . She never wrote me again."

Tony was grappling with the idea of whether or not he would come out alive. If he did come out alive, he was unsure of who he would be. Yet contrary to all that war attempts to do to the human spirit, the years that followed after Kasserine Pass brought out the finest qualities in his character—qualities that would leave him alive and certain of who he was during and after the war.

Photo sent from Muriel while Tony was in service.

CHAPTER EIGHT

After Kasserine: The Way Out of Africa

When Tony first sat down to recount his experience on these pages, his intentions were to share the stories that were most meaningful to him rather than provide a detailed chronology of his life and time at war. The stories that have been told thus far and those that follow herein are thus snapshots in time that remained significant to him over seventy years later, each for their own reasons. He felt that many of the stories needed to be told to express his gratitude for making it through seemingly impossible events and to honor the men who fought and often died beside him. Others needed to be told to show that despite the evil and chaos, there was a human side of the war that enabled the men to carry on through each day. The common thread binding all of his selected accounts were that they be told for the record, so that after his passing, future generations could learn and read about his experience.

In his words, "I didn't want to embellish too many operations about going up hills; going through the woods and brush; trying to cross riverbeds. Those things, I figure, were everyday happenings of war. We did the same things from battle to battle, from hill to hill, and from town to town to town. It was all repetition. The enemy had us pinned down; we pushed back; they got knocked off, so they moved back, and we moved up, same thing. So I figured, skip all that and focus on what was important."

The road out of Tunisia would comprise of fighting in the towns of El Guettar, Sened, Maknassy, Sedjenane, and Bizerte. Following the success of the Axis forces at Kasserine Pass, Allied commanders severely adjusted their strategy, seeking to emerge from the defeat with valuable lessons learned and vastly improved tactics. Among them were changes in leadership, including the introduction of George S. Patton as the new commander of the United States II Corps. Patton's campaign would take nearly three more months to complete, drawing much blood with much repetition, and conclude with the surrender of at least a quarter of a million German and Italian troops and a decisive Allied victory on the continent.

That long path to victory began just a few weeks after Kasserine Pass in late March 1943. The Anti-Tank Company travelled eighty miles south to El Guettar. Its orders were to join the Allied attempt to outflank the Axis front lines, driving the enemy troops into northeast Tunisia and inevitably ridding them from the continent. The extraordinary luck that surrounded Tony at Kasserine Pass was in fact just beginning.

As he began to describe in a grave recollection of his arrival at El Guettar, "We got there and no one told us the location of the Germans. We had to figure out everything on our own."

He remembered standing with a soldier on either side of him. The three men gazed into the distance looking for any sign of the enemy. The land was barren and empty. Most of the American troops were dug into foxholes, but German planes strafing overhead were slowly killing them. Additional enemy soldiers were positioned somewhere on the ground sighting and firing at the entrenched troops. Finally, Tony saw the flash of a weapon in the distance as a shell instantaneously struck alongside one of the soldiers next to him. The soldier to his left was decapitated and the soldier to his right was severely wounded. Tony was left unscathed. He stood there in disbelief and called for medics to help the wounded. Medics did everything they could to keep wounded men alive in this harsh and endless desert terrain. Unfortunately, even those men trying to save lives were not pardoned from harm.

~~~

Tony expounded upon another incident involving a neighboring company of the 39th Infantry Regiment. The company similarly had been sent into a forward position in the hills beyond El Guettar without any knowledge of the enemy's strength and location. They were hit hard behind German lines and their battalion commander was captured along with other members of the company; the aged commander had been an infantryman in World War I and Tony knew him from their shared time at Fort Bragg. As the remainder of this company was pushed back by the enemy, one of its platoons spotted an open crater formed from a previous battle and jumped inside for protection. Sadly, the Germans had already zeroed in on that location, suspecting that Allied soldiers would utilize the safe haven as such. Artillery shells were quickly fired onto that exact spot, killing and mangling the entire platoon in a single strike.

The Anti-Tank Company arrived later that evening and was thus spared from witnessing the disaster firsthand. They were ordered to replace the poor soldiers from the decimated platoon. Tony always told himself that if he made it out alive, he would never forget the sight of that platoon and how those men must have fought gallantly against the odds to their unfortunate end. He would remember how easily such a tragedy could have happened to any platoon.

~~~

After the costly victories in and around the towns south of Kasserine, the 9th Infantry Division was sent in an aggressive maneuver over two hundred and fifty miles to the northern tip of Tunisia at Sedjenane. Here Tony witnessed one of the more horrific memories of the campaign coupled with another instance of improbable fortune. The 4th platoon had been ordered to secure the high ground. As they moved towards the edge of a mountaintop to search for the enemy, Tony noticed something sticking out of the ground. Common practice in combat was to bury a fallen soldier in the field with his rifle in the ground as a tombstone, but this was something different.

Tony recounted, "It was an arm. A soldier was buried there. Instead of his rifle, they put his arm there. Maybe they used his rifle for someone that didn't have one. But all I saw was this arm, and yet we still had to do our job and see if the enemy was approaching the mountain."

Everyone resumed their duty in line and began taking their positions. Tony needed to defecate and went off to the rear of the platoon. He told the men he would be right back and dropped his pants to squat down. Moments later an artillery shell collided into the ground immediately beside him. It would have surely killed him, but it never exploded. Instead, the shell burrowed far underneath the ground leaving a long trail of raised earth.

As Tony detailed, "It must have been an armored piercing or a dud. I jumped because the thing hit so hard, and I watched it travel underground like a gopher. I pulled up my pants and I ran right back to the line. The shot may have been from the same enemy unit that killed the solider with his arm sticking out of the ground."

~~~

By May 1943, the United States had captured Bizerte and the British had captured Tunis. Prisoners were taken and the war in North Africa was over. Tony later reflected on the relative inexperience of the green American troops who matured so quickly to eventually succeed: "Sometimes I watch these stories on *The Military Channel* and I am reminded how precisely the Germans marched," he said. "When we were at Fort Bragg, we were a bunch of guys who would shuffle around half of the time. We were boy scouts, and they were military men from the very beginning."

As the American boys became hardened soldiers and the war effort progressed, life as they remembered it back home in the United States was moving on without them. Tony's sister Claire, nearly five years younger, was already engaged to her fiancé Jim. Claire wrote Tony constantly. As he penned to her on one occasion, "[Your letters] always come at the right time when I need cheering up and that's why I love to receive them all the more."

Claire mistakenly believed that Tony was coming home on leave in a few months and would be able to attend her wedding. She wanted to schedule the ceremony so he could be there. The Army would censor a soldier's outgoing mail and "black-out" any lines that could inform the enemy of a unit's location and future plans. In this letter dated June 8, 1943, Tony used his old nickname "Scotty," given to him in high school by his sisters' friend Viola, to secretly refer to himself in the third person and communicate to Claire that he could not be there for her wedding. Before doing so, he responded to the latest news on his beloved mother. She had recently taken up work with the Red Cross in an effort to support the children.

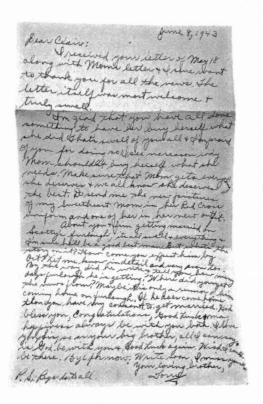

Dear Claire,

I received your letter of May 18 along with Mom's letter and I sure want to thank you for all the news. The letter itself was most welcome and truly swell.

I'm glad that you have all done something to have her buy herself what she did. That's swell of you all and I'm proud of you for doing so. I see no reason why

Mom shouldn't buy herself what she needs. Make sure that Mom gets everything she deserves and we all know she deserves the best. Do send me the new pictures of my Sweetheart Mom in her Red Cross uniform and one of her in her new outfit.

About you and Jim getting married on Scotty's furlough, it's all swell and everything and I'm sure he'll be a good best man. But what's the story on it? How come you expect him by October? Let me know in detail and very soon too. By the way, did he write and tell you how many days furlough he is getting? Where did you get the news from? Maybe it is only a rumor of him coming home on furlough. If he does come home then you have my consent to get married. God bless you, Congratulations, Good luck, and may happiness always be with you both. I love you, Sis, so as your big brother, all I can say is God be with you and Good Luck again. Wish I could be there. Bye for now. Write soon. I miss you all.

Your loving brother,

Tony

P.S. Regards to all.

Following victory in North Africa, the 9th Infantry Division travelled westward from Bizerte to the Algerian village of Magenta. Its location was situated eighty miles south of Oran and forty miles south of the French Foreign Legion Headquarters town of Sidi-Bel-Abbes. Although the break from combat was welcomed, living conditions for the men were insufferable. Temperatures reached one hundred and twenty-five degrees in the daytime, and flies engulfed the soldiers' eyes attempting to drain the fluid right out of them. Many of the men developed dysentery.

Tony was chosen to be in the Honor Guard, which comprised of two men from each company. Their responsibilities included the protection of dignitaries from England who came to North Africa to review and commend the troops.

On June 25, 1943, the Honor Guard was permitted to travel on a one-day pass to Oran. There Tony and the other men were afforded time to relax and enjoy the shops and pleasant scenery. At 10:00 p.m., they met their driver to head back in a caravan of trucks to Magenta. They were seated in an open-bed passenger truck just like the one from that first command post retreating towards Thala months ago. So much had happened since then that it seemed like another life.

The caravan weaved through the Atlas Mountains in the darkness. As they reached higher ground about fifteen miles south of Sidi-Bel-Abbes, someone heard plane engines and screamed, "Air raid!" Drivers were trained to quickly move off the road during an air or artillery attack to allow their passengers to safely disembark the vehicle.

"I guess our driver had one too many drinks waiting for us," recalled Tony. "He moved off the road all right, but this was the Atlas Mountains, there was no shoulder. All I could see were the tree branches hitting us as we plunged down the mountain. We dropped a hundred feet or more and flipped over coming to rest on the winding road below."

Many of the passengers were seriously injured in the crash. Tony remembered trying to lift parts of the overturned truck off the arms and legs of the other soldiers. Doing so made him aware of considerable pain in his shoulder.

Eventually, the truck was reached by another vehicle that drove down the mountain road to their position. Someone called for help and the next thing Tony remembered was being taken to a French Foreign Legion Prisoner of War Camp Dispensary. He had sustained a shoulder contusion and had bruises all over his back; his face was scratched up from the branches. He was strapped and medicated.

The next day, he was moved to the American 64th Station Hospital in Sidi-Bel-Abbes. The write-up of the story only reported that the truck had overturned. It neglected to mention how the truck slid off the mountain and the presence of enemy planes.

Right: Medical report detailing Tony's injuries from the truck accident on June 25, 1943.

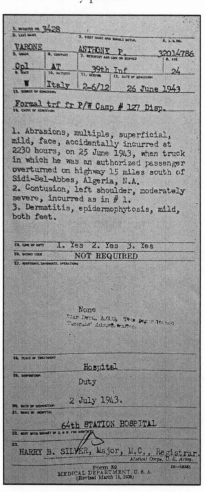

On July 2, Tony learned that his men were preparing for their next mission. He asked to be released from the hospital so that he could join them. The hospital staff told him that he could not leave until he was better. He had only been there for seven days.

"What happens then?" Tony asked.

"We'll send you out some place," the hospital attendant responded in a neutral tone.

"Where?" said Tony.

"Out to whoever needs you."

"Well, I want to be with my own outfit," he said emphatically.

"You can't go back now. Your shoulder's in a sling and you're all banged up."

Tony once more requested his rifle and uniform, and went on to prepare with the men of the 39th Infantry Regiment for their next mission.

Sicily loomed across the Mediterranean.

CHAPTER NINE

A Triumph For Optimism

Beginning in the early hours of July 10, 1943, one hundred and fifty thousand Allied troops landed on the island of Sicily in the sea and air invasion known as Operation Husky. The 39th Infantry Regiment went ahead of the rest of the Ninth to support the 1st Infantry Division, landing along the southern midpoint of the island. The invasion marked Tony's first return to his birth country since he emigrated to the United States at the age of three. British and Canadian troops fought along the eastern coast of the island, while the Thirty-Ninth travelled with other American troops along the western coast facing limited opposition from the Italian troops.

Ninety miles west of the landing site and three-quarters of the way to the western tip of the island, Tony found himself with members of the Anti-Tank Company in the town of Castelvetrano. Local residents surprised them by coming out of their homes with bottles of wine, bread, cheese, and dried sausage, attempting to convince him and the other soldiers to remain in the area longer than intended. The civilians further befriended the men with endearing Italian pleasantries. Tony sensed something was unusual and grew suspicious of his native people. He and his fellow men had not been treated with such generosity anywhere else during the war. He could sense the enemy watching them from a distance.

Soon all of the residents disappeared into their surrounding houses. Tony advised the men in his proximity to hit the dirt for cover. Italian troops opened fire with long-range weapons from an unknown vantage point. Tony's split second warning helped save the group from taking casualties. He and the other soldiers returned fire and narrowly avoided the ambush. The Allies eventually secured Castelvetrano and, after reaching the western town of Marsala, redirected east through the center of the island.

Victory in Sicily took just over one month to complete concluding with the surrender of over one hundred thousand Italian troops. Tony recalled encountering notable difficulty in the town of Troina. The terrain there was especially mountainous and they used donkeys to carry supplies and food because trucks could not effectively navigate the uneven landscape.

"Those poor donkeys worked hard," he reminisced, "but they sure would kick a lot."

Tony also fought on Mount Etna further east. He recalled being unable to dig foxholes because of its hard volcanic rock.

Somewhere along the way his first sergeant came over to him and asked, "Varone, did you lose anything?"

"No, why?" Tony responded.

The first sergeant tossed him a wallet. Tony had left it behind in North Africa when he hastily checked out of the 64th Station Hospital in Sidi-Bel-Abbes. Of course, the money that had been inside was long gone. Tony grinned, thinking how insignificant things such as money had become since being overseas.

Once they conquered Sicily, the Allies returned west to the town of Cefalu on the northern coast of the island, where they had an opportunity to restore themselves for a short while. The town had a beautiful cathedral offering solace, and the Mediterranean Sea for them to swim and relax. Life would ease for the next several months and provide Tony with reasons to be optimistic.

When he volunteered for the United States Army in October 1940, Tony knew that his service would make him eligible for American citizenship. He knew that one day he might partake in the country's promise for the pursuit of a brighter future for himself and his family. However, as harsh conditions and combat waned on him, such dreams slowly escaped his reality. He now considered himself fortunate to see each morning's rising sun; to eat a decent meal; to slip into a pair of warm socks; and to find a place to sleep where he would not be killed. He no longer consumed himself with elaborate thoughts of citizenship and the return to a normal life.

Three years after volunteering, Tony discovered that those forgotten dreams were soon to be reborn. On October 25, 1943, Corporal Varone became one of thirty-four members of the Ninth Infantry Division to be celebrated as naturalized citizen-soldiers during a special ceremony in Palermo, forty miles west of Cefalu. His service had earned him the right to a better life, and made him more determined than ever to return alive.

*Corporal Varone (front row, ninth from left) recognized as a
United States citizen at a special ceremony on
October 25, 1943[7] in Palermo, Sicily.*

On the evening following the ceremony, Tony wrote
a letter to his mother:

> *Somewhere in Sicily*
> *October 25, 1943*

My Dearest Mom: -

*Here I am once again telling you that I'm still in the
very best of health and feeling fine. I do hope you are
all at the peak of health and also feeling swell.*

---

[7] The official paperwork for Tony's United States citizenship was
completed on October 18. The formal ceremony occurred a
week later on the 25th.

Today I had my picture taken with about 20 other boys and my Division Commander. They also took a few notes on us boys and they said they would forward the notes with pictures to our hometown papers. Here's hoping you don't miss seeing the picture. You asked for a picture of me and I couldn't send one and now that I could, I couldn't get any made; so the papers in Brooklyn, such as the Brooklyn Eagle, and the Daily News, and New York Mirror will give you a chance to see me as I look today. I hope you can recognize me and I also hope you like the picture. Maybe I'll be able to send you a real photo of myself at a later date. I am still wearing my mustache, and my helmet had "AAA-O"[8] in white paint on it. Only three helmets had that marking on them, so it will be easy to pick me out. I also hope you like the story they will write about us.

Yes, Dearest Mom, today was another of those rare, happy, important, and unforgettable days for me and it means a lot for my future. And to make the day complete, I sent you a big package with Italian books for you; your letters; a souvenir pennant; a pair of swimming trunks that I used to swim in the beautiful

---

[8] Colonel Harry A. "Paddy" Flint assumed command of the 39th Infantry Regiment midway through the Sicily campaign. There he introduced the Thirty-Ninth to the slogan "Anything, Anywhere, Anytime. Bar Nothing." The "Triple-A Bar None" (AAA-O) symbol was etched onto all of their helmets and became a code to inspire them in battle throughout the war.

Mediterranean; two pillow cases; two lipsticks for the girls; two perfume bottles for you; five Holy Medals, one for each of you and one for my Beloved Dad – I have the sixth which means we all have one a piece; two souvenir stars from Italian soldiers' uniforms; souvenir coins; two Holy pictures; two souvenir rings from Biskra, Africa; and three handkerchiefs, one for you, Sweetheart, and one for Tillie and Claire. The trunks Fred can have if he wants and if he can fit into them. Well, Darling, it's closing time once again; so until tomorrow I say, "God Bless you and the kids." Regards to all. I'm always thinking of you, Dear Mom, and the kids. All my love and kisses are for you. Good night for now, Dear Mom.

Your loving son,

Anthony

The next stop for the 39th Infantry Regiment was the friendly territory of England. They embarked on a long sea voyage heading west from Cefalu for the Strait of Gibraltar, and then north towards Wales. They landed ashore on November 25, 1943 and travelled by train the remainder of the way to a military camp in Barton Stacey, England, where they would spend several months preparing for the invasion of France.

Here Tony was able to resume regular written correspondence with his family. On one occasion, he spoke of a particular fountain pen:

December 20, 1943
Somewhere in England

My Dearest Mom,

"Here I am once again with my trusty friend, my pen. I'll always cherish this pen and after the war when I'm home again, I'll sort of keep it as a treasure, for it is this pen that brings me closer each night to my loving Mom and my dear sisters and brother and to our true and real friends and relatives..."

Tony had found the pen on the ground in Tunisia not long after Kasserine Pass. He had heard from his superiors at the time not to pick up random objects because they could be booby-trapped by the enemy. Some went so far as to say that German planes were dropping pens during the night that would explode when a soldier attempted to use them. Despite the warnings, Tony acquired his pen and used it to write every single letter he sent for the duration of the war. He would get ink from senior officers that would last two or three weeks at a time. As foretold in his letter, he still has the same pen over seventy years later.

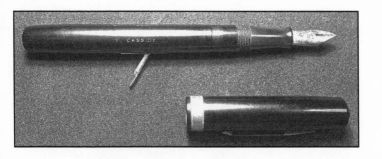

Pen found in Tunisia in 1943 and used to write all of Tony's letters for the duration of the war. – Photographed in 2013

In addition to writing his loved ones, Tony found other activities with which to spend his time in England. His most lucrative pastime was playing poker and twenty-one atop the bunks in the barracks at Barton Stacey. He still remembered some of his friend Arty's strategies from years ago in North Carolina and used them to his advantage.

He also found artistic outlets. His most memorable project was crafting himself a silver ring from a U.S. half-dollar coin. He worked on the coin every day for several weeks, rotating it perpendicularly along a potbelly stove while laboriously tapping its perimeter with his bayonet. After many patient hours, the tapped edges began to flatten and reveal the likeness of a ring. Eventually, Tony hollowed, smoothed, and perfectly rounded the coin to fit his finger. He held on to the ring throughout the war and for the rest of his life. A pawnshop once offered him four hundred dollars for it, but the ring was not for sale.

Tony formed this ring from a half-dollar coin in 1944.
— Photographed in 2013 —

Sentimental items such as the pen and this silver ring were more valuable to him than the money he had lost in his wallet and the money he amassed playing cards. They were tokens of consistency that brought him happiness and peace of mind in an ever more uncertain world. He had come so near death in North Africa and faced further danger in Sicily. England now represented a safer place for him. His character and personality were able to reemerge into the forefront and he was once again able to extract the positives from his past experiences. He could acknowledge the beauty of the Mediterranean. He could appreciate European architecture and the harmonious creations of humankind. Most of all, he could see a remarkable world waiting for him after the war:

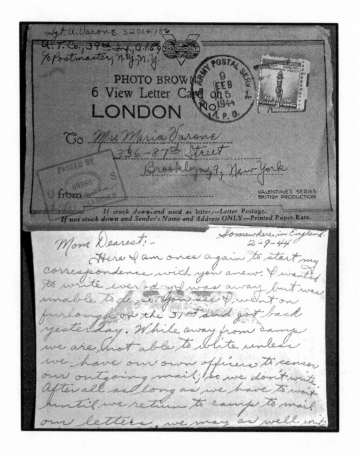

Original letter sent to Tony's mother on February 9, 1944.
The letter unfolded downward into several pages with the
scenic photographs that follow on the opposite side.

Somewhere in England
February 9, 1944

Mom Dearest,

*Here I am once again to start my correspondence with
you anew. I wanted to write everyday I was away but I
was unable to do so. You see I went on furlough on the
31st and got back yesterday. While away from camp
we are not able to write unless we have our own officers
to censor our outgoing mail; so we don't write. After
all, as long as we have to wait until we return to camp
to mail our letters, we may as well write them here and
have a little fun and do a little sightseeing while we
can. Right, Dear Mom? And so I did. I took tours
with the American Red Cross and I visited many
places during my four days in London, some of which
you see on the opposite side. Oh yes, the other four*

*days were spent in
seeing cities and
other places which
are on everyone's
"must visit list"
but for some
reason we are not
permitted to write
about it or them. Very picturesque, ancient, beautiful,
unforgettable, and important are all the places I visited
and someday I'll tell you and the kids all about them.*

You'll love hearing about everything from the corner pub (beer garden) to the House of Parliament. What beauty there is in England and this whole world of ours. Only to see them once is a feast to the human eye and to see them more and learn their history and story behind each and everything is an education and life well spent for everyone. Yes, Mom Darling, there is a lot to see and learn in this world of ours and the best way to enjoy and really learn is to see them. I think I'm going to set aside about two months in each year after I come home to travel and see the world and you, Dearest, will travel with me. Yes, Mom, we're going to see the world together and enjoy its true beauty. Maybe the kids and their husbands and wife and children would like to join us, I'd love to have them with us and I know they'll all gain by it.

Every afternoon I spent about four hours just sightseeing and how I loved it. Why, over some of the very streets you see in the pictures on the other side, I've walked over and stood on just to gaze and look in amazement and surprise. Yes, Mom Dearest, there are a lot of things I've seen up to date that I never knew were so strange to me, beautiful, different, etc. or that they even could exist. I can really and truly say that on my furlough I have enjoyed myself immensely and learned a lot about a lot. I also can say that there is a lot outside New York that New Yorkers never dreamed of.

113

And now I must close reminding you that I have thought of you every minute I was on furlough and hoped and wished you were here with me to enjoy it all. I am as always in excellent health and in perfect condition. I love you so very much, Dear Mom. God Bless you and the kids. Good night for now, I'll pray for you all, Dearest.

Your loving and devoted son,

Your Anthony

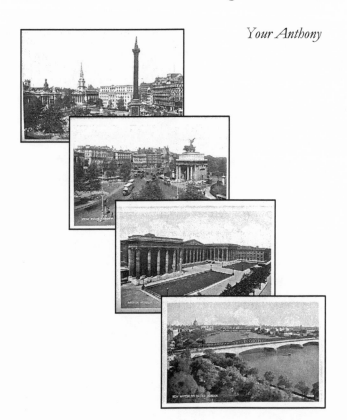

During the course of his correspondence with his mother, Tony received a photograph of her with the family's dog that would remain special to him after the war. Maria had struggled the first few years after Michael's passing. She raised Tony's siblings as a widow while managing the difficult emotions shared by all mothers with children in grave danger overseas. It helped that Tony never shared any of the hard times in his letters with her or anyone else for that matter. Nevertheless, it meant a considerable deal to Tony to see his mother's smile.

Maria Varone and Tony's dog "Babe."

On a lighter side, the photograph also made Tony nostalgic about another part of his civilian life: his dog. In 1939, a girl with whom Tony was acquainted gave him one of her dog's puppies as his 20th birthday present. Tony's family had their own name for the new pet, but Tony called her "Babe." The pup adored Tony and sometimes went so far as to help him in his romantic endeavors. When Tony saw an attractive girl walking down the street while taking Babe for a stroll, he would call out in her direction, "Hey, Babe! How you doing, girl?"

The object of his pursuit would stop furiously in her tracks and say, "Excuse me? What did you say to me?"

Tony would coyly explain that he was talking to his dog as Babe responded extra playfully leaping about. Ten minutes later, he and the young lady would still be chatting away rather pleasantly. Although his canine companion could not join him overseas, Tony's antics soon resumed once in England.

Over weekend passes, Tony often took the one-hour train from Barton Stacey into London. During his second visit, Tony noticed an attractive girl walking down the street and approached her. Her name was Lana and she was a few years younger than him. She agreed to go on a date with him that evening.

"We had a nice time that night," Tony recalled. "We went to a pub that had not been bombed or anything.[9] Then we found a restaurant that was still going. The whole thing was casual. 'Well, thanks for spending time with me. And nice meeting you.' And we parted. We didn't even schedule another date."

On his next visit, Tony met a Canadian soldier with whom he started paling around over the course of the next several weeks. The two would go to pubs together and explore the town.

As Tony recounted, "One day I was waiting for him at the bus stop and I spotted Lana stepping off a bus. I said to myself, 'Wow, look at that girl. She's nice!' And then I realized it was Lana. I kept waiting for my friend to come, but in the meantime I was talking to her. And we just chitchatted about things. She said her two brothers had fought in Africa like I did. They were both military men. She also had a sister named Edna who was in the Women's Auxiliary Air Force and would come home every weekend on pass like me. The family had a lot of money. One thing led to

---

[9] The notorious bombings of London known as "The London Blitz" had occurred several years earlier on (from September 1940 until May 1941) and prior to the United States entry into the war. However, another significant campaign (Operation Steinbock or "The Little Blitz") began in late January 1944 while Tony was in England and continued for several months.

another and I said 'Well, I got a friend here,' because I was trying to leave. I didn't want to hangout with her that much. I figured she was a good-looking girl and the next thing I know she'll be dating some other guy. I didn't want to get choked. I figured I would let it pass. So I said 'I got a friend here', but then she fired right back 'Well, I got a sister.' So I asked my friend if he would go out with her sister and he said 'Sure'. And we all went out together the next time we were in town and from then on."

Tony saw Lana every Saturday he could. They would dine together and go for walks gazing in amazement at the devastation of the bombings that had taken place. Tony eventually met her parents and often joined them for dinner at their home. Edna and Tony's Canadian friend did the same.

One weekend Tony fell asleep on the train back to Barton Stacey. He woke up when the train came to a stop at a nearby town beyond Barton Stacey. He recalled today with a smile on his face, "I didn't know where I was going. I knocked on a door of some guy's house like crazy. It was maybe twelve or one o'clock in the morning. Finally there was a window upstairs and the guy yells out, 'What the hell are you knocking on our door for?' I said, 'I'm in trouble. I missed my stop and the train took me here instead of the American Barton Stacey camp. Which way is it to get back?' He said, 'Go down that road right there. You'll meet it. But it's about eight miles down.' So after partying around all weekend and on little sleep, I said to myself 'Okay, I'll walk like I did with Arty back in the Carolinas.' But this time I had to make sure I got there in time. I didn't fall asleep or anything. I got back around 5:00 a.m. and all was alright."

Despite Tony's weekly encounters with normalcy, the terror of the war was ubiquitous in London. The United States was fortunate to have its homeland so physically distant from the war. The same could not be said for Great Britain. A number of times Tony visited Lana, frightening sirens sounded off in the streets of London alerting the citizens of an approaching German air raid. As he described, "Everyone would scramble out of their homes and go down into the subway because that was the safest place. People would be crying as they went carrying infants in their arms. When they came out, some of their homes were blasted away."

One evening, Tony and Lana were on a date in a movie theatre when they again heard the sirens. Everyone ran out of the theatre except for them. They looked into each other's eyes with faint expressions of bravery, and smiled sincerely as the movie continued rolling in the empty theatre. They told each other without words that they did not have to run, for everything that mattered to them was in front of them and if they should die together so be it. Their love for each other was growing, and Tony had not felt such emotions since parting with Muriel by the ink of his pen in Tunisia.

As his personal life became restored, Tony equally excelled in the Army. Within his first few months in England, Corporal Varone was promoted to Sergeant and made one of four squad leaders for the 4th platoon. In future combat, this rank would permit him a greater leadership role and the freedom to go about on his own exploring enemy terrain.

He was also among those specially selected to train with British Commandos for a period of several weeks to learn their tactical methods and intelligence for the impending landings in France. It was his duty to pass that knowledge onto his company. Training took place in Bournemouth and the Isle of Wight along the southern coast of England.

As time passed, Tony and Lana came to acknowledge that their weekends together would soon come to an end. With the Ninth expected to set sail at a moment's notice, Tony snuck Lana into the camp one night at Barton Stacey to say farewell.

"We went out into the area beyond the barracks," he described. "We talked all night and the next thing I knew my unit was on alert and I had to get her out in a hurry. I got her out past the guards at the gate. They must have seen her and turned a blind eye. Then she took a bus to the train and went home. That was the last time I ever saw her . . ."

Lana would send Tony letters and photographs throughout the war, and he would continue to write to her nearly every week. Her departure that evening in Barton Stacey signaled the next turning point in Tony's journey. Six months since arriving in England, the 39th Infantry Regiment was now destined to reenter combat. Ahead of them was the colossal challenge that they had prepared for throughout Africa and Sicily, and one for which the 9th and 1st Infantry Divisions would be the most combat-experienced.

Lana

– September 1944 –

CHAPTER TEN

Entering the Main Arena

Jutting out conspicuously halfway along the northwestern coast of France is an area of land called the Contenin Peninsula, part of the geographical region known as Normandy. In 1944, the Allies famously coded the beaches along the eastern border of this peninsula with the names Utah, Omaha, Gold, Juno, and Sword. On June 6, "D-Day," thousands of ships carrying tens of thousands of American, British, and Canadian soldiers, many of whom had never before seen combat, crashed into waves of relentless enemy fire and onto those fateful beaches to initiate one of the most significant military invasions in modern history. The landings were a superb planning effort by all involved, with elaborate calculations, tedious preparation, and most significantly, the inescapable sacrifice of thousands of lives in the pursuit of a noble mission on behalf of humankind.

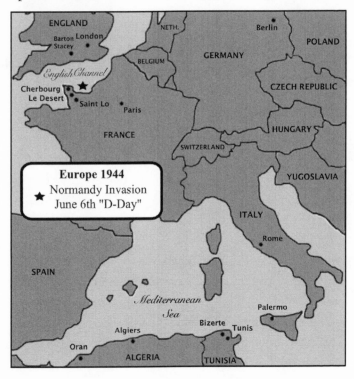

Nested at the center of the northern edge of the peninsula was the city of Cherbourg, containing a critical harbor that when controlled would provide the Allies with an entry point for ships carrying the troops, supplies, and equipment needed to support the liberation of France and inevitable march on Germany. On June 10, D+4, the 9th Infantry Division sailed across the English Channel and landed at the most western of the five beaches, code-named

Utah. The Ninth's mission was to spearhead an invasion that would rapidly cut westward across the peninsula, isolating enemy troops on the peninsula from the main forces of the German army further inland. The mission would also include the eventual capture of Cherbourg, thirty miles north.

**Path of the 39th Infantry Regiment
--- June 10 – July 18, 1944**

As Tony recalled, "We moved so fast that the enemy never saw us coming. We left a part of our division to hold the line while we moved on to the harbor of Cherbourg. It was a long and tough fight but we accomplished our mission with great success. The German forces surrendered in large numbers and we freed many American prisoners. We left some GI's to hold the position, and engineers to clean up the harbor and prepare it to accept needed supplies and reinforcements."

During the mission, the 4th platoon of the Anti-Tank Company was attached to the 39th Infantry Regiment's 1st Battalion, fighting alongside Tony's former outfit, Company C. The 1st Battalion later received a Distinguished Unit Citation for extraordinary heroism on June 18. Members of the 4th platoon were equally awarded. Tony does not often speak of the encounter, as one of the many young soldiers who died beside him was from Brooklyn and had volunteered for the Army on the same day as him in October 1940. Their unspoken bond made the loss resonate deeper in Tony's heart.

After taking Cherbourg, the Ninth travelled southeast. They were destined for Saint-Lo, where the 1st Infantry Division and other units were struggling to push through enemy lines and liberate more territory. Several weeks had passed since landing on Utah Beach.

In the early hours of July 11, German tanks from the notorious Panzer Lehr Division launched a surprise counterattack on the 9th Infantry Division troops as they slept in the rolling hills and hedgerows[10] outside

---

[10] The landscape in this region of France was made up of hedgerows. Each hedgerow was upwards of four feet high with shrubs and trees on top. They ran parallel to each other and were separated by open fields. Sightlines between opposing sides were severely impaired, as was the mobility of troops and equipment.

the village of Le Desert. The Germans were attempting to escape the peninsula and return to their main forces, and the Ninth and its fellow Allied units were blocking their path. After several desperate hours and heavy casualties, the Ninth regrouped with orders to establish new defensive positions. The various companies amid the battlefield initiated their respective procedures of engagement with whichever men were still able to fight. An executive officer from the Anti-Tank Company ordered his jeep and two 2½-ton trucks to be assembled. He directed the lieutenant and platoon sergeant of the 4th platoon to load up all four squads and move out to confront the Panzer Lehr assault.

One of those squads was led by Sergeant Varone. Riding in a truck, Tony mentally drifted back to the Kasserine-Thala road as he tried to fathom how the fifty men from the 4th platoon could be expected to inflict material harm onto the German tanks. The executive officer escorted them to the base of a hill in front of the enemy's position. He instructed the lieutenant to lead the men up the hill on foot and establish a defense. The executive officer would remain in his jeep with the trucks and drivers along the road.

The four squads moved swiftly up the hill where they sighted a series of hedgerows. The lieutenant charged towards the first hedgerow with two squads following closely behind. Suddenly, a deafening shot rang out as he was spotted by an enemy tank. The shell landed next to the lieutenant launching lethal shrapnel in all directions. He dropped heavily into a foxhole as another soldier beside him was badly wounded.

Tony sprinted over to the foxhole and lifted the lieutenant by the front of his uniform. The brave soldier's body was now lifeless. The blast had killed him instantly. The wounded soldier beside him was the leader of another squad. He was severely bleeding from his leg.

In Tony's words, "I looked for our platoon sergeant who was next in command. When I did not see him, I immediately took over the platoon. I told the men to take positions against the hedgerow and to keep five or six feet apart. Once more, I directed them to fire from multiple positions while moving from right to left and left to right. I told them to throw as many grenades as possible as fast as they could, and give the enemy every reason to believe we were a much larger force than we were. I placed the light machine gun team in the middle, a bazooka team next to them, and riflemen on both sides. I told them to keep firing while I went to tell our executive officer to call for medical help and reinforcements."

As he rushed back towards the road, Tony found his platoon sergeant taking shelter in an upright foxhole formed into a hedgerow. The soldier was frozen with a blank stare and a pistol in his hand.

"I ordered him to go help the men of our platoon," Tony commented, "but he turned a deaf ear and looked towards the ground."

Tony continued towards the road at the bottom of the hill where he found his executive officer still sitting in the jeep. Tony promptly informed him that their lieutenant had been killed and one of the squad sergeants wounded. He asked for the officer's support in leading the men against the German tanks and infantry.

"I can't leave these trucks," responded the executive officer. "I have to be ready to move you out if you get pushed off."

"For crying out loud, we're going to get pushed off if you don't help us!" pleaded Tony.

The executive officer radioed for a medic and reinforcements, but would not abandon his trucks. As Tony readied himself to return to the onslaught, another vehicle pulled up alongside them. The soldier in the passenger side asked them how the situation looked up ahead. Tony quickly noticed that the soldier was a United States Air Force officer.

"We could really use some help," Tony said eagerly.

"Well, that's what I'm here for," replied the officer.

"Can you get an airstrike on my position if I show you where we are?" Tony asked with desperate resolve.

"You bet!"

Tony was flushed with hope for the survival of the 4th platoon. The officer handed him two rolls of orange-colored material that would each be about three feet wide and eight feet long when unraveled.

"I'll call in the airstrike and tell the pilots to look for these orange markers," said the officer. "Lay them in front of your position and the pilots will strafe and bombard the enemy ahead of you."

"I would do that sir," Tony said cautiously, "but the Germans are in the next hedgerow. If I go out in front of our position, I'll be killed before I lay those markers. I'll place them behind our position instead."

"Very well," replied the officer. "I will instruct the

pilots to adjust accordingly."

Tony thanked him and hurried back up the hill. He passed his platoon sergeant once more in the foxhole. The frightened soldier waved Tony on with no intentions of rejoining the platoon.

Returning to the battle, Tony told his fellow soldiers the good news and to keep firing as he laid down the orange markers. Within minutes, they could hear the sound of plane engines overhead.

"Here they come!" shouted Tony. "Guys! We got it made!"

The bombs descended forward through the air and practically over the heads of the American soldiers before landing directly onto the German tanks in the next hedgerow. The powerful impact of the explosion lifted Tony's prone body nearly two feet off the ground and knocked his helmet off his head.[11] It was a minor price for being rescued by the United States Air Force. The platoon was jubilant.

---

[11] Like many GI's, Tony never buckled his helmet during combat. He had been told disputed stories of soldiers caught in proximity to explosions being decapitated or sustaining severe neck injuries due to the intense pressure of air forced into their fastened helmets. Given the variety of dangers in his path, Tony chose to take every precaution he could, regardless of how improbable a particular threat may have been.

The scene in the next hedgerow could not have fallen into greater contrast. Tony solemnly recounted the dismal image before his eyes as he approached the defeated enemy: "We moved forward and started to take prisoners. They looked stunned, dazed, frightened, and whipped from the bombing. Some tank operators were burning while hanging lifelessly from the tank turrets; others were blown to pieces. Those alive didn't know where they were at. We stripped them of their weapons and anything they could hurt us with."

Two additional companies from the 39th Infantry Regiment soon arrived to relieve the soldiers of the Anti-Tank Company and guard the prisoners. Having suffered casualties in the battle, the tenacious squads of the 4th platoon returned to their trucks with mixed emotions. Their executive officer led them in his jeep back to the company.

"My men told me that I did a great job leading them through such a tough time," Tony said nostalgically. "They said they would follow me anywhere, and they did just that. We stayed as a team to the end of the war. I felt good knowing that everything turned out well. I prayed that our lieutenant would rest in peace."

Despite holding off a collection of German troops and making it possible for the Air Force to bomb and strafe the enemy to its end, the 4th platoon never received recognition from their company nor the U.S. Army. Neither did Sergeant Varone.

The soldier who sustained the leg injury from the explosion that killed the lieutenant was awarded a Purple Heart for his wounds. Tony heard much later in life that the same soldier also received a Silver Star and promotion to staff sergeant for the events of the day. He had never fired his weapon. Tony suspected that his own actions were misattributed to the wounded soldier since both he and the wounded soldier were squad sergeants with Italian heritages.

The platoon sergeant who hid in the foxhole eventually rejoined the group, and neither he nor the executive officer in the jeep reported the platoon's heroic actions to the company commander. Another battalion of the 39th Infantry Regiment who fought that day was recognized with a Distinguished Unit Citation for similar feats.

"I do not know who took the glory, but not we who fought off the attack," Tony said with many years of acceptance in his voice. "I never bragged about my deeds. I felt it was our senior officer's duty."

Back with the Anti-Tank Company, the men of the 4th platoon were fed and rested. They considered what was ahead of them, with expectations of further difficult fighting to come soon enough at Saint-Lo.

Less than twenty-four hours after the battle, Tony reached once more for his faithful pen to write another letter to his mother. In what had by now become standard practice for him, Tony did not reveal the slightest sign of the terror that he had so recently experienced. His fear and suffering remained buried between the lines and imperceptible to an unknowing loved one. While he could not withhold his longing for home, his focus remained on the health and well-being of his widowed mother and her children:

July 12, 1944
Somewhere in France

My Dearest Mom:

Here I am once again to let you know I am still in excellent health and in perfect condition as always. I am also very lonesome for you and I seem to miss you more and more every day. Mom Darling, I also want to remind you that not a day goes by without my thoughts straying away to you. Yes Sweetheart, I'm forever thinking of you and the rest of the family and most of all I'm loving you, Dear Mom, as much as ever if not more.

Well, Dearest, how are you and what's new on the home front and with the kids? I pray you and all are in splendid health and as happy as possible and taking extra special care of yourself for me as I am doing for you all.

I received your lovely and most encouraging letters of June 27, 29 (AM + PM), 30, and July 1 and I do thank you from my heart. You're a wonderful Mom and lovely all the time. I'm happy to learn that you are receiving my mail. Thank God for I was afraid you would worry over me for no reason if you didn't get my letters. I'll always try to write at every possible opportunity...

... And now I say, "Don't worry, my Beloved Dad will pray for me along with you and the kids, and God will guide me and protect me always and bring me home someday safe and sound to you. My regards to all and kisses to you and the family.

Loving son,

Anthony

Tony later described the logistics of his correspondence with loved ones while overseas. Incoming letters would arrive roughly every three to ten days. He kept his outgoing letters in his mess kit because the metal would provide protection from the rain. Whenever he had a moment, he jotted down a few lines, picking up where he had previously left off.

In this manner, Tony wrote his mother once more a few days following his letter of July 12. Here he reflected on his past campaigns with that same glaring omission of hardship. The realities of war emerged, however, when he responded to a question from his mother about Lana:

July 17, 1944
Somewhere in France

Mom, my Dearest –

Hello once again and how are you? Fine and in perfect health as usual, I pray. And the kids, what's new with them and how are they? Also in very good health and happy as possible. As for me, Dear Mom, I'm still in the very best of condition and in excellent health as always.

I received your extra special and very lovely letters of July 3 and 4 today and I was very pleased to read all the interesting and good news.

About France, yes, it is a lovely place and I like it a lot, but you know the old saying, "there's no place like home." Of course, England was beautiful; Sicily was grand with lots of fresh warm air and shining sun; Africa had lots of strange things along with hot sun and blistering sand and an occasional cool and refreshing oasis, but the U.S.A., Mom Darling, has and always will have the best and most beautiful everything there is, mostly because it has you and the family and my home. The French people are pretty swell though and from those I've talked to and seen, I can understand why they wanted to be liberated and free. One more thing about them is that they'll give a soldier nearly everything especially old wines and cognac. Yes they're pretty swell alright and deserve to be free again. When we get some time off or a pass I'm going to visit the historical places and interesting cities and learn all I can about every place and everything and then I'll write you a nice long letter and tell you all about it.

You ask about Lana and so I'll write about her. The reason why you probably didn't hear from her as yet is that she has been bombed out and her home has been destroyed. Her family and herself are now at her sister-in-laws house and will be until they find a new home. For a long time they were living in their air raid shelter and sweating it out. Ever since we left there for the invasion the no good Nazis have been bombing them with their darn "doodlebugs"[2] and killing and destroying those poor people and their homes. It makes us fight all the more though because we know [Hitler's] just no good and deserves the worst beating of his life for harming the civilians all over the world. We know he does for we saw a lot of cases of destruction, etc. to the civilian population of the countries and places we've already been to. The Nazis are just no good through and through.

With all that bombing and until her house was totally destroyed, Lana kept writing to me very often and as often as possible. She's pretty swell, Mom Darling, a real trooper.

About Eddie,[13] I'm praying for him to get a furlough real soon for he deserves it. Yes, my brother, now a daddy. I can just picture him bouncing Tori on his

---

[12] Following the Allied invasion of Normandy, the Germans began sending V-1 flying bombs into London. Also known as the "doodlebug" and "buzz-bomb" because of the sound of its engine, the V-1 was shaped like a small plane and could travel considerable distances before landing on a pre-determined target. The Germans launched nearly ten thousand V1's into Britain in the aftermath of Normandy. The attacks killed approximately six thousand British citizens and wounded seventeen thousand over the course of several months. Fortunately, many V1's were unsuccessful due to faulty design.

[13] Eddie was Tony's childhood friend from Brooklyn who was now serving in a Coastal Artillery Regiment for the National Guard defending the harbors of New York. His wife Florence recently gave birth to their first child.

knee and looking real good, proud, and happy, especially with Florence. They're a grand couple. I know he'll be home to see you and I know you'll have a real nice spaghetti and meatball dinner ready for him. Right Sweetheart?

And now Dear Mom, I must close until tomorrow or real soon when I'll write again. God Bless you, and give my regards to all, also be sure to give the kids my love and a big kiss. Take care of yourself for me, I'll do the same for you. Don't worry about me. I'm always thinking of you, Dearest Mom, and loving you devotedly.

Lovingly yours, your son,

Anthony

Lana sent Tony a photograph of her sister Edna in front of the family's destroyed residence. Her mother was the only member of the family who was home when the bomb struck. She survived by the good fortune of being on the opposite side of the house from the site of the blast. Tony imagined the experience must have been horrific. Indeed, it was simply another instance of the war's indiscriminate path of suffering and devastation.

Lana's sister Edna in front of their destroyed home. – 1944

Meanwhile in France, the 9th Infantry Division had since become entangled in the carnage at Saint-Lo. Fighting in the vicinity of this village was the stage for many unfortunate events. In one instance, poor weather conditions led to an unexpected and disastrous blunder whose bitter image has remained with Tony throughout the years.

A hot climate through the prior spring and summer had scorched the battlefield. The Allies and the Germans controlled opposite sides of a road in combat gridlock. An American airstrike was radioed in and the first round of aircraft swiftly arrived to bombard the German position. The initial bombs crashed onto the arid land releasing a tremendous amount of dust into the air. Heavy winds then shifted the dust onto the American position. The next round of planes arrived and naturally believed their target to be beneath the now displaced cloud of dust. Many American lives were lost in the friendly fire.

"So the enemy stayed put and was safe, and instead we got bombed," Tony recounted.

One of the Ninth's most beloved soldiers to fall in the vicinity of Saint-Lo was Colonel Harry A. "Paddy" Flint. Despite his age, the fifty-six-year-old commander of the Thirty-Ninth was regularly seen leading his troops into combat. On July 23, Flint was struck by a sniper's bullet moments after riding atop a tank being sent in to support troops like Tony on the front lines. The commander died the next day.

Leadership of the Thirty-Ninth was passed on to Lieutenant Colonel Van H. Bond. A few days after Flint's death, Bond issued the following letter to his troops in which he quoted solemn lines once penned by their deceased commander. The words of both men were indicative of the unnatural but necessary mentality surrounding the loss of life in war. Tony's original typewritten copy remains in his possession seventy years later:

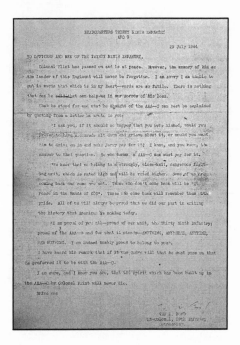

HEADQUARTERS THIRTY NINTH INFANTRY
APO 9

29 July 1944

TO OFFICERS AND MEN
OF THE THIRTY NINTH INFANTRY,

Colonel Flint has passed on and is at peace. However, the memory of him as the leader of this Regiment will never be forgotten. I am sorry I am unable to put in words that which is in my heart – words are so futile. There is nothing that can be said that can help us in our sorrow of his loss.

What he stood for and what he thought of the AAA-O can best be explained by quoting a letter he wrote to you:

"I ask you, if it should so happen that you were nicked, would you prefer to have a comrade sit down and grieve about it, or would you want him to drive on in and make [the Nazis] pay for it? I know, and you know, the answer to that question. He who harms a AAA-O man must pay for it.

"We know that we belong to a strongly, close-knit, dangerous fighting unit, which is rated high and will be rated higher. Some of us are coming back and some are not. Those who don't come back will be "At Peace in the Hands of GOD". Those who come back will remember them with pride. All of us will always be proud that we did our part in writing the history that America is making today.

"I am proud of you all – proud of our unit, the Thirty Ninth Infantry; proud of the AAA-O and for what it stands – ANYTHING, ANYWHERE, ANYTIME, BAR NOTHING. I am indeed humbly proud to belong to you."

I have heard him remark that if it was God's will that he must pass on that he preferred it to be with the AAA-O.

I am sure, and I know you are, that the spirit which has been built up in the AAA-O by Colonel Flint will never die.

Drive on!

Van H. Bond
Lt-Colonel, 39th Infantry
Commanding

Final victory would require more lives to be lost. It would require more families to receive more letters filled with words incapable of alleviating their suffering. It would require the lives of more mothers and fathers, newlyweds, brothers and sisters, sons and daughters, to be shattered in the name of a greater good and a higher purpose — the brave and humble sacrifice of the military family.

Tony continued to focus on what he could control. He had always done the best he could and had succeeded thus far. Now it was time for him to follow through on his personal mission of survival.

CHAPTER ELEVEN

The Eleventh Hour

Following Saint-Lo, the Allies pushed relentlessly across France and into Belgium. In September 1944, the 39th Infantry Regiment breached the German border for the first time at the city of Roetgen. The next six months contained some of the longest and costliest battles of the war. They would become yet another eternal source of untold accounts of heroism and tragedy that fell with their respective soldiers into the abyss of war.

The Thirty-Ninth crossed the Siegfried Line and fought gallantly through the nightmare of the Hurtgen Forest (Rhineland) before being called back and forth into Belgium to help defend against Germany's final offensive in the Battle of the Bulge.

145

Tens of thousands of American soldiers laid down their lives upon each battlefield. The significance of their sacrifice and the courage in their hearts cannot be overstated. The fear that engulfed the seasoned veterans, let alone the thousands of replacements who were experiencing combat for the first time, cannot be made any truer with words upon a page. It is to speak of the intangible, raw emotion surrounding the moment that an individual's existence is called into question against horrific odds, and no words or image can recreate such emotion for the sympathetic observer. Sergeant Varone and the other fortunate souls who managed to survive struggled to comprehend how they still were on this earth.

In his words, "You can't fathom what goes through your mind. You say to yourself, 'This is the day it's going to happen.' Or the guy right next to you gets killed, and you ask yourself, 'Was that meant for him or for me?' And rather than answer you just think to yourself, 'It's going to happen to me any day now, but I'm going to get as many of them as I can to make up for the guy they hurt on my side, or this other guy, or the guy behind me.'"

Tony was later awarded a Bronze Star Medal (First Oak-Leaf Cluster)[14] for meritorious service in the

---

[14] Oak-leaf clusters are small metallic pins issued to soldiers who have received the same medal on more than one occasion. They

Rhineland. He regarded his actions as part of the "everyday happenings of war" — the repetition of battle that he alluded to during the final push out of North Africa. Some things are best left unsaid.[15]

The physical and mental obstacles facing the soldiers intensified over each passing week, and German combatants were not the only source of opposition. The winter months of the campaign introduced nature's harshest elements. Soldiers were often forced to sleep outside on the frozen ground or in foxholes. They sought shelter in deserted buildings whenever possible. Such refuge came in the form of abandoned military homes, hospitals, garages, shops, and private residences, sometimes half-destroyed from prior attacks. The men rotated who guarded their sleeping quarters throughout the night.

Occasionally, locations thought to be empty were inhabited by elderly families, or women and children who remained behind while their husbands were in combat. These could be unfortunate human beings

---

are affixed to the cloth of the original medal. A "First Oak-Leaf Cluster" indicates the second instance of the same award. A "Second Oak-Leaf Cluster" would indicate the third, and so on. Tony received this award in 1959, which by that time marked his second Bronze Star Medal.

[15] Tony's cousin, Private Anthony M. Varone of the 101st Airborne Division, died fighting south of Bastogne, Belgium. He was posthumously awarded the Silver Star Medal.

trying to hold their families together, or potential threats, as encountering armed and hostile civilians was not uncommon. Every so often, isolated children as young as ten years old suddenly appeared from around a corner armed with rifles, engaging a squad of soldiers caught off guard.

Sharing with deep sadness in his eyes, "You think to yourself, 'How can I shoot that little kid?' But he's going to hurt you or one of your guys. You don't want to do it, but it has to be done."

The men were further tormented by the knowledge that non-military items such as chairs and wooden crates could potentially be booby-trapped by the enemy prior to their arrival. Some Germans knew English and would attempt to trick the American GI's, shouting, "Hey Joe! Is that you?" If a soldier realized that there just so happened to not be any Joe's in his outfit, he was fortunate; other times perhaps not. Such impersonations could lead to the ambush of an entire squad. All of these elements served as psychological weights for them to bear, forcing them to second-guess everyday movements, gestures, and interactions.

By early March 1945, the 39th Infantry Regiment reached the town of Bad Godesberg, located along the western bank of the Rhine River, fifty miles east of the Belgium border. The Allies had been struggling to find passage across the Rhine as the enemy systematically destroyed its own bridges to prevent Allied advancement. Sergeant Varone was ordered to lead his squad on a nighttime patrol to gather intelligence on enemy positions, strength, and numbers. He was not to engage the enemy unless fired upon.

Key Events: September 1944 - March 1945

In the early hours of March 7, the squad returned to the company command post and Tony relayed his report: He had encountered several American units during his nighttime patrol, and observed German artillery pieces firing in the direction of Bad Godesberg from points south and west. He also spotted German infantry units throughout the area.

It appeared the Americans were precariously situated

between a divided enemy. On one side, a defeated horde of German troops was pulling back from points west of the Rhine. On the other, the enemy's main force was firmly defending the Rhine's eastern bank. The stage was set for a battle.

Tony's platoon leader ordered him to quickly deliver his latest intelligence to the battalion command post. There he would receive orders as to where the company should position itself and lay mines to prevent enemy assaults from the rear.

When Tony reached the battalion CP, he began placing pins onto a map to show senior officers where the enemy was positioned. Suddenly, a radioman rushed over and cried out, "The 9th Armored Division tankers just captured the Bridge at Remagen! In tact! We need everyone we can to help hold it!"

The vehement soldier was referring to the Ludendorff Bridge, located in the town of Remagen about ten miles south of Bad Godesberg. It was their last reasonable hope for crossing the Rhine and moving further into Germany. Enemy soldiers had wired the bridge to explode but had been unsuccessful in their efforts thus far. Tony was ordered to return to his company command post and rush all available riflemen to the bridge in support of the 9th Armored

Division. They were to cross over to the eastern bank and set up a defensive position, known as a bridgehead, on its northern side.

Before Tony could respond to his orders, the battalion command post fell under a barrage of heavy artillery shelling. There were some German prisoners being held in a barn next to the CP who began to escape. Another soldier shouted for support rounding them up. Tony helped recapture two prisoners.

The barrage resumed and Tony resolved that his top priority was returning to his company and reaching the bridge. As he dashed through the shelling, the blasts increased in proximity and he knew that he needed to find cover if he wanted to be anywhere at all. He darted beneath a large truck parked in line with others alongside the road. The trucks were transporting tall stacks of deflated pontoon boats intended to be used to cross the Rhine.

As he braced himself in a prone position, an enemy shell landed right onto the truck and exploded above him. It was a direct hit. The reverberating sound of the explosion was momentarily deafening. His body rattled violently in the confined area between the ground and the truck's underside as his face and chest smashed into the dirt. A considerable amount of blood started flowing out from lesions in and around his mouth.

Tony patted his hands against his face and chest. His injuries were only flesh wounds; he had survived again. The explosion surely would have been fatal if not for the layers of pontoons that absorbed the impact. He briefly remained beneath the burning truck in shock and disbelief until the flames grew too hot to withstand. Then he quickly collected himself and rushed to his company command post.

In his words, "Knowing the importance of my orders, I forced myself to obey. I emerged from underneath the truck and moved cautiously but hastily. I ran into another sergeant who saw that I was bleeding heavily from the mouth and chin. He said I should seek medical help as soon as possible. I told him I had no time and had to get my men over to the bridge. I knew that if we failed we were going to have a hell of a time crossing that river. Holding the bridge would bring us a step closer to final victory. It meant less loss of life, and maybe seeing home again sooner."

Back at the company CP, Tony's platoon leader ordered him to move out in a pair of small trucks with two squads. By the afternoon, they had reached the Ludendorff Bridge. The impressive steel railroad bridge was constructed in 1918 and spanned nearly a quarter of a mile from Remagen to the town of Erpel on the eastern shore of the Rhine. A pair of cylindrical stone towers resembling a fortress flanked the entrances on both sides. Heading towards Erpel, the tracks led into a large tunnel cutting through the base of the Erpeler Ley Mountain adjacent to the Rhine.

In his words, "Upon arriving at the bridge, we were told to drive across slowly and heed warnings of explosive devices that were being defused by engineers under the bridge. We were reminded that the enemy was now on the high ground in force and did not retreat as we had hoped."

Tony led the two squads onto the bridge to help the many other gathering Allied units secure the bridgehead. They were greeted immediately with a heavy assortment of enemy fire. Halfway across and praying for a safe passage through the onslaught, Tony witnessed the first German jet-engine plane he had ever seen shoot across the air. It was faster than the Messerschmitt that had strafed his men in Kasserine and any other enemy aircraft up until this point. His eyes swiveled across the sky searching for a bomb. Then suddenly, he spotted a shell ripping through the air. He was unsure if it came delayed from the jet or was just another artillery shell, but such details were irrelevant. Images of Le Desert flashed through his mind: orange markers, decimated tanks, wounded men. This time he would be on the receiving end.

The bomb struck the top of one of the towers on its way to the ground and shrapnel rained down over the bridge. The majority of the men around him were badly wounded. Some were killed. Miraculously, he and a few others were unscathed. He quickly gathered himself and dismounted from the truck to survey the wounded.

Charging back and forth under enemy fire, Sergeant Varone helped nearly a dozen wounded men into the main tunnel at the base of the Erpeler Ley where medics were waiting to treat them. Most of the men had shrapnel in their backs, arms, and legs. Carrying them into this area afforded them protection from the enemy and desperately needed care.

Tony gathered the handful of remaining men who were unharmed to set up a defensive position. Enemy shells continued to strike the mountain and a position of higher ground could not be readily established. Instead, the men shuffled down into a culvert underneath the southeastern side of the bridge. They lined up shoulder to shoulder with their backs against the wall as shrapnel began to ricochet into the culvert. One soldier would have been hit in his hip but his canteen, suspended from his waist, absorbed the impact. Given the proximity of the shrapnel, another soldier directly in front of Tony instinctively started to move to the opposite wall of the culvert for better cover. The idea seemed good at the time.

"I was about to go with him," Tony solemnly recounted. "I was halfway across when a piece of shrapnel hit the guy in the side of the head. It went in one side and out the other, and the blood poured down. He was such a good guy, too."

The shelling ceased and Tony took a moment to wash himself with water from the Rhine. It was becoming difficult to distinguish other men's blood from his own. The soldier who was killed by the shrapnel was his friend and one of his best soldiers. A few months earlier, the man received a letter from his wife asking for a divorce. These incomprehensible things happened when men were at war for this long. The soldier never had time to take her off his insurance policy, so she received the financial compensation following his death instead of his parents.

The remaining men in the culvert eventually emerged and ascended the northern side of the Erpeler Lay to secure the high ground. They nervously awaited the unpredictable hours that followed. Sporadic fire continued throughout the long day, but luckily a counterattack never blossomed.

On March 10, Tony and his men were relieved by supporting infantrymen and returned to the Anti-Tank Company. An enormous number of Allied troops and supplies were able to cross the Rhine before the bridge finally collapsed on March 17. Temporary pontoon bridges were constructed and the Allied campaign in Germany narrowly avoided a significant setback thanks to the courageous efforts of its soldiers.

A lieutenant later reported Tony's actions at the Ludendorff Bridge.[16] Tony was awarded the Bronze Star Medal with "V" device, the United States military's fourth highest award for valor, in recognition of his carrying eleven wounded men to safety.[17] The honor was bittersweet as it was a permanent reminder of his friend's death in the culvert and the others' on the bridge.

Tony never saw a medic for the wounds he sustained under the truck at the battalion CP, and thus precluded himself from receiving the Purple Heart.[18] In his words, "Once I got across the bridge and was

---

[16] The report mistakenly cited March 10 instead of the 7th.

[17] This was Tony's first of three Bronze Star Medals. The second and third were received years later for meritorious service (Rhineland) and a citation in orders (Combat Infantry Badge).

[18] The Purple Heart is awarded to soldiers who are wounded or killed in combat. Recipients are required to present official medical and military records detailing the incident.

helping the guys who were really hurt, my injuries were the last thing on my mind; yet time and time again, I managed to escape death."

HEADQUARTERS NINTH INFANTRY DIVISION
A. P. O. #9

201 - GNMEQ   9 May 1945

SUBJECT: Award of Bronze Star.

TO   :   Commanding Officer, 39th Infantry,
          9th Infantry Division, APO 9, US Army.

          Under the provisions of Army Regulations 600-45, as amended, the Bronze Star is awarded to:

          ANTHONY P. VARONE, Sergeant, 32014786, 39th Infantry, who distinguished himself by heroic achievement in action against the enemy on 10 March 1945 in the vicinity of Erpel, Germany. During the crossing of the Ludendorf Bridge spanning the Rhine River, an enemy artillery shell burst directly in front of the vehicle in which Sgt. Varone was riding. With complete disregard for personal safety, he immediately dismounted from the vehicle and assisted in the evacuation of eleven casualties to the nearest Aid Station. Sgt. Varone's aggressive initiative and courageous actions were instrumental in saving the lives of several of the wounded and were a credit to himself and to the Armed Forces of the United States. Entered military service from New York.

          By command of Major General CRAIG:

                                        G. L. MATERKIEWICZ
                                        Major, A. G. D.
                                        Acting Adjutant General.

DISTRIBUTION:-

   2-39th Inf
   1-Sgt. Varone
   1-AG File

Sergeant Varone receives the Bronze Star Medal
with "V" device for individual heroism during the crossing
of the Ludendorff Bridge. – Awarded May 1945

On April 12, 1945, President Franklin Delano Roosevelt died from failing health at the start of his fourth term in office. He had led the United States from the depths of the Great Depression and through the war, but would be unable to bear witness to the final outcome of his nation's efforts. Meanwhile, the 9th Infantry Division had battled nearly two hundred miles east from the Rhine River to the city of Nordhausen. The loss of their Commander in Chief had been a tremendous shock to the troops, who would only be shaken once more by the horrors they encountered in this city only days after his death.

Located in the heart of Germany, Nordhausen was the site of a Nazi extermination camp. The camp had been mistaken by the U.S. Air Force as an enemy target and regretfully bombed in early April. It was then liberated by the 104th Infantry Division and 3rd Armored Division a few days prior to the Ninth's arrival. For the first time in the war, Tony encountered the stark realization of the nightmare that he had until this point only heard gruesome tales or seen unsettling pictures from intelligence operatives while fighting in other countries; those stories and pictures were now realities in the foreground with real victims, living and dead, and those still-living enemy prisoners of war responsible for their atrocities.

As Tony recalled, "The Nazis tried to defend the camp because they didn't know we had pushed their army back as far as we had. Any chance they could fight us, they would. The survivors looked like ghosts in clothes. We fed them and did everything we could to help them."

Hitler killed himself on April 30 and Germany formally surrendered on May 7. Although war in the European Theatre was nearing its end, those closing weeks of April still contained some notable engagements for Sergeant Varone:

One memory in particular from this period occurred during an afternoon in the vicinity of the Mulde River. Tony was walking along a road near a military police (MP) outpost. His rank of squad leader since landing in Normandy nearly one year prior afforded him the liberty of initiating patrols both on his own and with his men during breaks in the action. He was alone on this occasion, several hundred yards beyond the MPs, when he noticed a vehicle wandering in his direction. It was an enclosed enemy transport bus. He stood firmly with his rifle drawn, signaling the driver to pull over. The bus slowed but failed to stop as its distance from him gradually diminished. He fired one or two rounds into the ground ahead of the front tires to ensure that his gesturing was understood as a demand and not a request. The bus abruptly pulled to the side of the road and became trapped in a small ditch.

Tony slowly approached the vehicle. Its passengers were a handful of German officers, including a general. They had pistols but were otherwise unarmed. Their nonthreatening disposition suggested that they no longer wished to fight and were attempting to reach the safety of their own lines further east. A blown bridge had in fact forced them to take a detour. Now they were cornered.

In a futile attempt to circumvent the situation, the general nonchalantly leaned out from the vehicle, gesturing for Tony to help push the bus back onto the road. Tony looked at him with amusement. Perhaps the general believed that a casual response to their predicament would somehow enable them to pass, or, in a show of hubris, that a lone American sergeant was not capable of bringing them in. Regardless, Tony told them to get out of the bus and push it back onto the road themselves. His plan was to use the vehicle to transport them to the MPs.

As the officers filed out, Tony noticed a couple of younger GI's in the road and yelled over to them for assistance. He made a squad of them. Together they disarmed the prisoners and checked the luggage for additional weapons, supplies, and items of intelligence. The prisoners' English was largely poor except for one subordinate soldier who proved to be an effective translator. The bus could not be extracted from the ditch so Tony instructed them to gather their belongings and march towards the MP outpost. As they moved forward, the soldiers grew visibly anxious. They called on their translator to learn more about their fate. The general, an older man in his mid-to-late fifties, was the first to speak. He asked where they were being taken and if they were due to be executed. Tony assured them that they would only be transferred to a POW camp and not be harmed.

The austere general took a deep breath and exhaled. Then he glanced to his side and gestured to his bag. The translator said to Tony, "He says that he won't be needing that anymore and would like you to have it." Tony maintained a defensive stance with his rifle. He had briefly inspected the luggage earlier, but motioned for the prisoner to open the bag in question once more. Inside was nothing more than a spare uniform and a few daggers. The exchange seemed indicative of an unwritten ritual of which both Tony and the general understood the significance. Each of them aspired to escape the war. If the decision were up to the two of them, the war would have ended right there. Tony handed the German officers over to the MPs and took the bag back to his platoon.

In Tony's words, "I suppose we could have shot them, but I didn't want to do that. It's one thing if they're fighting back, but these guys were captured. I just didn't want them going back behind their lines and contributing to any more American casualties."

That evening, Tony studied the uniform more closely. Medals and insignia indicated that the officer was a two-star general, or "*generalleutnant*," who had served in World War I and on the Eastern Front in World War II. Examining the uniform accentuated the similarities between American and German principles of training, organization, and reward systems. Considering the mirrored experience of fear and suffering on the battlefield further connected both sides into an unspoken brotherhood. It was the salient contrast, however, between the objectives to which those principles and experiences were applied, that shattered all notions of comparison.

The uniform marked the second occasion that Tony acquired enemy paraphernalia. He had also removed a large Nazi flag draped from the top of a captured building in an overrun town. Being in the Army for nearly four and a half years brought some advantages. When thoughts of taking home a few keepsakes crossed his mind, he could always depend on his old friend Henry to carry out such a request. Henry was a corporal who worked in the supply room. Although sending home such paraphernalia was discouraged by the military, some remembrances of a hard fought journey were too meaningful to leave behind. The corporal arranged for the items to travel by land and sea to a final destination in Brooklyn, New York.

Several weeks later, a package arrived at Maria Varone's doorstep. Tony was still in Europe. His mother opened the mysterious bundle to find an enormous Nazi flag covered in what she believed to be blood. Unbeknownst to her, seawater in the cargo hold at the bottom of the transport ship had leaked into the package. The flag had been used to wrap the German general's daggers, which rusted and stained the flag with a sporadic brownish-red residue. Maria was startled and frantically washed the flag to remove the "blood." As concerns of her son's safety and thoughts of his experiences flooded her imagination, she placed the washed flag where she hung all of her wet laundry, on the clothesline extending into the courtyard outside her apartment building window. Neighboring windows surrounded the small courtyard on all four sides. Within minutes of the flag coming into sight, shades were closed and blinds drawn. As in a scene from a black-and-white war parody, Maria inadvertently frightened the entire building.

Meanwhile in Germany, Sergeant Varone and the 39th Infantry Regiment were headed to meet Russian troops at the Elbe River. This union signaled that the United States had secured the Western Front and the Soviet Union had secured the Eastern Front. He still remembers watching those comrades from the East celebrating with vodka on the opposite side of the river. The only drink available to Tony and his fellow men on the western side was water. Still, that water quenched his thirst like nothing had in four years. It signified the closing of a period in his life that he never imagined he would survive, and the beginning of a cherished lifetime that would now come after. He could sleep better and dream better. Home was on the horizon at last.

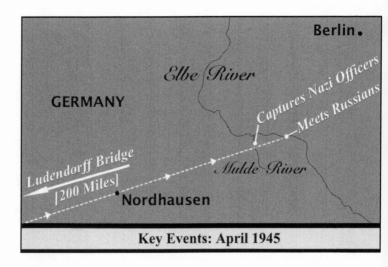

CHAPTER TWELVE

All This For Ordinary Men

"Sergeant," said his company commander. "You've done a great job here. How about joining on with our boys in the Pacific?"

Tony was speechless. Thirty-one months had passed since he sailed across the Atlantic destined for England. The Army was beginning to send soldiers home based on the points system. Those who had accumulated eighty-five points were eligible for discharge. Tony was granted one point for each month in service, and five points for each award, decoration, and campaign star. Surviving eight campaigns over the course of thirty-one months, plus the twenty months he spent in training, had alone earned him the right to go home. Adding his individual medals, and the many awards earned by his regiment, ratcheted his final tally well over the minimum.

Tony respectfully declined his commander's request to volunteer for additional combat against Japan. He would never know if that decision saved his life.

In lieu of combat, the month of May provided Tony with a well-deserved opportunity to travel Europe. He initially expressed dissatisfaction over the mandatory furlough, which separated him from the men with whom he had spent the entire war. Once on the road, however, Tony seemed to enjoy everything just fine. A letter to his brother Frederick written on May 29, 1945 detailed his experience.

His eighteen-year-old brother had recently joined the U.S. Navy. Freddie would spend his months of the war on an aircraft carrier in the Pacific where he was responsible for directing plane traffic on the flight deck. Tony had urged his brother to join the Navy over other branches of the military. Serving on a Naval vessel would at least provide Freddie with a dry bed and proper rations. He would not have to spend his time battling frostbite in the snow and trekking through mud like an infantryman.

Somewhere in S. Germany
May 29, 1945

Dearest Freddie:

I received your long and excellent letters of March 11, 25, April 11, 16, and 25, and they made me most happy. It pleased me greatly knowing that you are in the very best of health as I hoped you would be. Good knowing you got my letters on your return . . . I'm so pleased that your leave turned out so pleasant and that you and the family all enjoyed your stay at home.

Say Brother, I guess I'm through fighting for a long while now but I know you'll take over and carry on doing what you have to and that's all . . .

. . . I don't think you know about my 25-day furlough so I'll tell you a bit about it. I left Dessau near the Elbe River and crossed it trying to contact Russian patrols. We captured thousands of Krauts who had very little fight in them (knocked it out of them) and then continued on. Well, the job was good and well done and we did run into the Reds. Boy they are wild and do they go to the limit with the drinks.

Two days before it was over, I was chosen as the first enlisted man in the battalion to go to the Riviera on furlough and the very first from the company. I spent nine wonderful days there . . . Then it was Luxembourg City for a while, then Verviers, then Spa and a few other places here and there to make my furlough the very best deal yet.

While I was on furlough I missed the first group to leave for discharge, for I have lots of points and I am right up there in the upper brackets. The second group left and I still missed it by a day for I got back to see them off. Then the third group was picked and I was right up there in the lead so I'll make it this time unless I get word on my England furlough to marry Lana. I hope I get there right soon so that her and I can come to the States together and I pray more than anything that you won't leave for the Pacific for a long while yet. I hope you go on a couple of months of maneuvers and get back home in time to welcome me and get yourself another furlough.

By the way handsome, your snapshot is swell and I sure do appreciate having it. All the guys think you're grand and very attractive. I think you're the very best, tops, and I didn't see a single sailor to compare with you. Wish I had your looks and personality. Why, it's the best yet and no question about it. I'm a bit jealous and afraid that maybe Lana will try to marry you when she sees you. What a man you are.

Well Freddie Dear, I must close this letter, but I'll write again soon and let you know how I make out. God Bless you and Good Luck always. I know our Beloved Dad will guide you and pray for you and our Good God will protect you and bring you home again soon, safe, and sound back into civilian life. Then we'll really make up for the time we were apart. Pray for Dad. Take good care of yourself and remember, I'm always thinking of you, love you, and miss you so darn much. Regards to all your mates and everyone. Thanks again for the letters and photo. Hope you forgive me for not writing sooner and more often. I'll do better, I promise.

Your loving brother,

Tony

See you soon.

Tony and Lana had written each other consistently throughout the war as they had promised each other on their last night in Barton Stacey. They intended to be wed in England, however Tony was never granted the furlough. Instead, he was assigned to return to the United States with that third group of soldiers he had mentioned in his letter to Freddie. The couple's future together was once again uncertain. Although Tony was understandably dismayed, his already improbable life's journey would encounter a wonderful turn of fate in due time.

Returning to the United States from Germany was not as simple in the 1940s as by modern standards. Tony recalled being driven from Germany to Paris, where the soldiers spent a memorable week in a city overflowing with celebration. They then flew to the Azores Islands off the coast of Portugal to refuel before crossing the Atlantic.

Tony in Paris on his way home to the United States.
– June 1945 –

For the main leg of their journey, the troops were transported in a plane generally used for American paratroopers. They sat shoulder-to-shoulder with their backs against either side of the hollow fuselage.

Guys were quiet and smoking a lot. Midway through the flight, the pilots decided to have some fun at the expense of Tony and his fellow passengers.

"Gee Bill," said one of the pilots to his co-pilot loud enough for the boys in the back to hear, "I heard another one went down this morning. That's three this week. They're really asking a lot of these old planes."

The poor troops had survived the entire war, and were now being led to believe they could die in a plane crash. There was of course no danger, and the returning soldiers would reach North America safely. Prior to landing, the pilots made up for their practical jokes by inviting the soldiers to join them in the cockpit, a few soldiers at a time, to gaze at the rare and miraculous view of the sun setting over the Atlantic Ocean. Painting the horizon with rays of red, pink, orange, and yellow, this glorious end to their journey carried an internal peace that further symbolized their escape from the war. Once on the ground, the soldiers were transported to Presque Isle, Maine, where they spent a couple of days before boarding a train headed for Fort Dix, New Jersey.

Maria's oldest son had reported for training on her birthday, January 16, in the year 1941. He returned home four and a half years later, on June 27, 1945, two days before his twenty-sixth birthday. His sister Tillie borrowed a car to pick him up from Fort Dix.

The drive into Brooklyn felt like a dream. Vivacious color and renewed perspective immersed his abstract memory of home that had since faded into black and white. Tillie parked the car and Tony emerged from the passenger side outside of a physical home for which he had no memories. The family now lived on 82nd Street between 5th and 6th Avenue. As he approached the front door, he first recognized the sound of his pup Babe going wild for him, with the strangely familiar pacing of her paws and whimpers of excitement. She smelled him long before he walked in, and the photographs had not lied for she was no longer a pup. She would live for eighteen years in all.

Tillie and Claire were both recently married in April and June of 1944. Claire had waited another eight months for Tony to be able to attend after she received his "Scotty" letter, but the war carried on. Tillie was now twenty-three and Claire was twenty-one. Tillie and her husband lived with Maria. They had a newborn son; Tony was an uncle.

"I was invited to the weddings," he remarked lightheartedly, "but would you believe the Army wouldn't let me come?"

Tony understood that the family dynamic had changed significantly since 1941. In addition to a new home, new marriages, and brothers at war, the most obvious difference was of course the absence of his father Michael. Time overseas helped Tony find peace with his father's passing in a way unlike the rest of the family. Physically isolated from all of his loved ones, Tony could emotionally carry his father's spirit and memory with him through the most difficult moments of the war, without having to face the realities of his father's absence from the familiar places and routines of day-to-day life in Brooklyn.

The unifying figure for Tony upon his return was his mother. All of the changes had revolved around her for they were made up of her husband, sons, and daughters. As a result, she was the most recognizable symbol of home. She was the binding matriarch who had weathered each challenge life tossed her way and carried on with strength and resolve. When he walked through the front door for the first time in so many years, he and his mother knew that their embrace was a sacred moment that hundreds of thousands of mothers and sons just like them had not been fortunate enough to share.

Despite his family's love and support, Tony's return to life in the United States became psychologically burdensome over time. The nation was still at war with Japan and would be until August. While initially optimistic about his future, Tony experienced a gradual decline in his mental health as he began to feel invisible, ignored, and misunderstood by a society that he felt could not comprehend the horrors that he and his fellow men had faced, and the monumental task that they had accomplished for their country.

The Servicemen's Readjustment Act, better known as the G.I. Bill, had been signed by President Roosevelt in June 1944 to support a soldier's transition into civilian life by providing funds for medical care, unemployment insurance, higher education, and housing. Freshly home from the war, Tony was eager to pursue his dream of a college education, which his family had been unable to afford upon his high school graduation in 1938. When he inquired with the Army, he was told as per the G.I. Bill, that funds were only approved for those whose education was "impeded, delayed, interrupted, or interfered with by reason of his entrance into the service." Since he was not enrolled at a university when he volunteered for service, Tony was precluded from the benefit.

Readjustment managed to be difficult in matters as rudimentary as shopping. Soldiers wore government-issued clothing throughout their time in service. Thirty days after returning to civilian life, however, they were no longer permitted to wear their uniforms. When Tony left for the Army, his mother passed the majority of his civilian clothing onto his father and brother. Tony thus had limited options upon his return, and purchasing a new wardrobe turned out to be more of a challenge than he expected.

"You had to have ration stamps," he explained, "and I didn't know I was supposed to go to this place to get them in order to survive.[19] Nobody told me, not even at Fort Dix where we mustered out: 'Okay, you're free! Go home. Here are your papers.'"

One rainy night, Tony went to a store to see if he could acquire a pair of shoes. He had been wearing his Army boots up until this time. A middle-aged police officer was standing inside the store with his hands in his coat pockets, modestly seeking refuge

---

[19] The Office of Price Administration (OPA) was a federal agency established during World War II to prevent wartime inflation. The agency set ceilings on the prices of consumer goods and rationed items that were in higher demand than the available supply. Such items included sugar, gasoline, coffee, and particular types of food and appliances. They also included rubber-made goods such as tires and shoes. Each citizen was given a ration book containing ration stamps. When purchasing a rationed consumer good, customers were required to present the proper stamp prior to purchase. The goal was to ensure the fair distribution of scarce resources as the nation and the world committed itself to the war effort. The OPA existed until 1947.

from the rain. Tony entered the store, and soon approached the counter with a regular-looking pair of shoes and sufficient payment. Adhering to federal regulations, the storeowner requested Tony's ration stamp. Tony explained how he had never picked up a ration book and recently returned home from the war, but the storeowner adamantly refused to sell him the merchandise. Tony continued to plead with the gentleman, so much so that the police officer overheard the commotion and began walking towards the counter. The intimidating lawman looked at Tony, who grew noticeably anxious, and then directly at the storeowner.

"Hey Mac!" exclaimed the officer. "This kid here is a veteran. Give him a break will you?"

The policeman then turned to Tony and said tactfully, "Here, take my stamps."

Tony was relieved. He greatly appreciated the unexpected kindness. Still, the twenty-six-year-old was demoralized by his own inability to accomplish the simplest of tasks. On the battlefield, he had successfully led his men through circumstances of life and death. Here at home, he could not navigate the purchase of a pair of shoes. Such a welcome home was not what he had envisioned. He felt alone. He sensed ingratitude. He was increasingly vulnerable.

In his words, "Even my mother and my siblings thought I was a little off when I got home. I wasn't really [off] . . . I wasn't *happy* . . . I was sad . . . Sadness of friends lost . . . Sadness of things seen . . . Feeling like just another ordinary person . . . A lot of my guys were still in Germany and I didn't know whether or not to write them. So I became more or less like a recluse. And it stayed with me for a little while. But, I managed to overcome."

Trapped between two worlds, Tony shut himself indoors and resorted to alcohol. He emerged into the neighborhood by routinely going out with one of the few familiar soldiers with whom he flew home from Europe. They frequented old Brooklyn bars like the Shore Road Casino, Hamilton House, and McGuff's.

Necessity, combined with the resilience of his character and support from his family, inspired him to take his first positive steps forward and ascend from his dark state in the later months of 1945. He reignited the work ethic that propelled him through his childhood and high school years by partnering with a friend on the purchase of a radio store in South Brooklyn for a two-hundred-dollar initial investment. The investment eventually proved unsuccessful, however it led to him and his brother Freddie, who had since returned from the war, meeting a man who was able to set them up with a job. They became unionized longshoremen on the Brooklyn docks, loading and unloading ships along the waterfront. It was hard labor. Workers would line up early each morning to be selected for assignments. Not every man was chosen. Tony and his brother's contact in the union ensured they were picked each morning on account of them being veterans.

Eventually, the work of a longshoreman became too rigorous and Tony opted to pursue a job with Bethlehem Steel in the Brooklyn Navy Yard. He mainly functioned as a pipefitter, working in the bottoms of ships that needed repair. He also center-punched the names of ships onto their bows by hanging over the side from a boatswain's chair. The center-punched stencil outlined where another worker would later paint the name of the ship onto its bow. All Tony could think about was how he had survived the war but was going to fall thirty feet off the rope-suspended chair and onto the dock and break his neck. Some evenings everyone went home and there he was hanging in the chair working all by himself. He and his brother did everything they could to find work and keep a roof over their mother's head. On the weekends, Tony worked as a *Good Humor Ice Cream* man in a white suit. He amassed simple pleasure in making the children happy.

In 1946, he obtained a job as a home improvement salesman for the Olson Company, which specialized in roof work, siding, and insulation. The job was based on commission, and Tony was eventually promoted to sales manager.

During this time, Tony was hired to perform work on the home of a man named Jerry. It just so happened that Jerry was the uncle of a young lady with whom Tony went to high school. Her name was Viola. She was the gal who had nicknamed him "Scotty" and befriended his sisters ever since the morning she asked Tillie about the upperclassman who walked Tillie to school.

Through all the years, Viola never forgot about Tony and their few dates in high school. Tony had always kept things friendly between them, and then began dating Muriel towards the end of high school. Viola knew Tony's relationship with Muriel was serious, so she kept her distance, and did not write to him while he was in service. She followed her own path of romance, yet still managed to stay up-to-date on Tony's life over the course of the years thanks to her strong relationship with his sisters.

In high school, the three girls went dancing together every Wednesday, Saturday, and Sunday at the Loews Theatre on New Utrecht and 46th Street. Entry cost them each a quarter. They had a wonderful time playing the jukebox and sipping on chocolate soda drinks until their midnight curfews.

After high school, Viola worked as a receptionist at a dress company and a nursing home company. She still lived in the Brooklyn home where she was born and raised at 167 Dahill Road, right next-door to her Uncle Jerry's. When the United States entered the war, Viola volunteered to help build weather instruments for the Army in Long Island City. The instruments used human hair inserted into a device that was lifted into the sky by balloon to collect information on the moisture content of the air.

In Tony's words, "Being that Viola was friends with my sisters, she was at my home a few times after I returned from the war. I was always sitting in a room watching TV or something, and she would say hello and ask how I was. She kept coming over to see Tillie, and in the meantime she was trying to catch me. Well, after I worked on the job for her Uncle Jerry, I decided to ask her out on a date and that's when I started breaking out of my depressed state."

Tony and Lana had continued writing each other once he returned to the States, but Tony decided that he needed to live in the present. Reaching London from New York by telephone was too expensive for him to afford even a few minutes of conversation, and the cost of physically travelling between the cities was astronomical. His feelings for Lana remained strong, but he could not sit at home all day thinking about the war. So he made up his mind to date this bright and cheerful girl from a time in his life when everything seemed better. Viola and Tony began seeing each other once a month, and soon enough once a week, which before long was every day. Her optimism and love for life was contagious, and Tony's affection for her became self-evident.

After a few months, Viola learned about the international competition for the object of her affection. As Tony recalled, "She told Tillie, 'I really like your brother. I'm going to marry him.' Even my belated father had told her years earlier, before I started dating Muriel, 'Yeah, you're going to marry my son.' Italians make arrangements for kids. One thing led to another and Viola got a hold of Tillie one day and said, 'What's this? Why is this girl Lana always writing him?' And Tillie said, 'Well, she wants to marry him. She has her visa and everything.' And Viola said, 'Well I want to marry him too!'

"All at once I didn't get a letter from Lana. I said, 'What's going on?' So my sister told me that Viola wrote Lana a 'Dear John' letter. She told Lana we were dating! And then later on Viola told me, 'You're not going to hear from her anymore, I wrote her a letter!' . . . I guess girls have a certain way of doing things."

Fate indeed has a unique way of working itself out. Tony and Viola found increasing happiness together over the next two years, and soon enough marriage entered the conversation. As Tony recalled, "It was just one of those things where she said sweetly, 'You know we've been keeping company for two years. Are you going to get serious? Are we going to get married?' I don't remember how I worded it, but I said 'Sure!'"

On March 28, 1948, Tony and Viola were married at Bay Ridge United Methodist Church on 4th Avenue and Ovington.[20] The date was deliberately chosen in honor of his father's birthday. Three years prior to the wedding, Tony had been fighting in Germany from the Bridge at Remagen towards Nordhausen. His mind in March of 1945 could hardly imagine that such a wonderful day was waiting for him if only he survived. The day meant all the more to him because he did.

---

[20] The couple was actually raised Catholic, but March 28th fell on Easter Sunday of that year and no Catholic church would conduct a wedding ceremony on the same day.

As newlyweds, Tony and Viola followed a similar trajectory as when Tony's parents were first married, living in various rental apartments over the next ten years in Brooklyn. They started out in his mother's apartment before moving to different flats on Church Avenue, 86th Street at 3rd Avenue, and East 7th Street.

While living in these last two apartments in Brooklyn, Viola gave birth to their two children. The couple's first child, Rick, was born on September 19, 1952. He was named after "Richard the Lionheart," the 12th century English king and warrior, because Tony loved the stories he had been told of Richard I's courage and leadership. Their second child, Michele, was born on October 4, 1954. She was named in honor of Tony's beloved father, with the single "l" to mirror the Italian spelling of Michael.

In the future, both children would proudly serve their country, with Rick in the United States Navy during the Vietnam War and Michele in the United States Army shortly thereafter. Both would be honorably discharged and go on to have families of their own. Rick and Michele would each bring two children into the world, and Michele's children would collectively welcome four more. Michele's son would serve proudly for the United States Marine Corps in Afghanistan in the wake of 9/11 and be honorably discharged. All of these lives and their stories could have so easily been erased had Tony been killed during the war.

Tony and Viola's two children, four grandchildren, and four great-grandchildren (thus far) are a microcosm of the hundreds of thousands of families whose similar exponential possibilities of life and happiness were taken from them upon a battlefield some seventy years ago. Thankfully, the story of Tony's family goes on.

By 1953, providing for one newborn and planning to conceive another, Tony and Viola were struggling with the inconsistency of Tony's commission-based income. One week would yield a substantial paycheck while other weeks would leave him without enough to cover their basic expenses. He decided to pursue a more stable career and secured a job as a salesperson for the Blessings Corporation, which delivered diapers and linen supplies to homes and hospitals.

Each summer, Viola and her mother rented a home for the extended family on Lake Ronkonkoma, located at the center of Long Island. As the destination became increasingly crowded over the years, they began visiting family in Lake Panamoka further east instead. Each weekend, Tony drove all the way back and forth from their East 7th Street home in Brooklyn while Viola entertained the children on the lake throughout the week.

Viola in Long Island.

One Sunday while driving home from Long Island, Tony encountered heavy traffic in Smithtown. He turned down a random road leading to Kings Park, which eventually led him onto a particular street with new homes for sale. Rather than remain in traffic, Tony chose to pass some time looking at the homes. After a while, he realized that he actually really liked them. In an act of spontaneity, Tony put down a ten-dollar deposit on a house. He later phoned his astonished wife to tell her that he had bought them a new home. While they were not approved for that particular house, Tony's initial move led to the eventual purchase of the two-story home on that same block, where they have lived since 1955.

There are long, seldom-mentioned hours and nights between bouts of combat where a soldier is quietly and unsettlingly left alone with his thoughts. Ten years after surviving the war, Tony had amassed all that one could have hoped for during those restless hours and nights. He had a quaint suburban home with a loving wife and two young children whom he would be able to watch grow up and raise families of their own. He had the beginnings of a stable career and the opportunity to experience what civilians might too hastily refer to as an ordinary life, but what veterans like Tony, who in their darkest hours grew to cherish life's simplest pleasures, knew was so much more.

The remainder of his life would, like any other, be filled with pleasant and less pleasant times. Similar to the years prior to the war, however, the years that followed provided Tony with a myriad of experiences that later made for wonderfully entertaining stories, colorfully and articulately recounted in his unique style. One in particular, which came full circle from his childhood, addressed the inanimate former accomplice of Tony's that happens to be featured in the portrait found on the cover of this book: the cigarette.

For the majority of the 20th century, most people did not understand the harmful effects of tobacco. Highly effective advertising campaigns coupled with situational factors of the times allowed the unhealthy habit to evolve into a largely acceptable social practice. Tony's smoking began at the disturbingly young age of seven, when he began picking up unfinished butts off the street. It was the same year that he was struck by the yellow taxicab, so perhaps he had a greater need than most seven-year-olds to settle his nerves.

He recalled a memory of being caught smoking by his father Michael while his age was still a single-digit. Tony flung the cigarette into the street in a futile attempt to escape punishment as he simultaneously repressed the excess smoke inside his lungs with his lips sealed. Tony's father walked sternly over to his son. Making the youngster suffer for a few moments with the presumption of being in the clear, Michael finally spoke.

"Alright, let it out!" he said.

Tony comically exhaled and gasped for air. He was strictly grounded, but the sentence was not enough to break his habit. He smoked for thirty-three years, with a disproportionately greater amount of it during the war.

The random and nonsensical occurrence that finally liberated Tony from his inclination came on a day of fishing in 1959 with his son Rick, who was coincidentally seven years old at the time; Tony was forty. In Tony's words, "It was that little lake in Smithtown. I was baiting my son's hook and letting him throw the line. 'Whoops! The fish got that one.' So I'm baiting it again and there I am smoking all the while. I had a mustache at the time, and the same hands I was holding the cigarette with were also touching the bait. And I realized that if I didn't smoke, I wouldn't have to put these fingers to my mouth. But being that I do, I'm touching my mustache and getting all of this bait, and fish, and dead stuff all over me. It was disgusting! So right there I said to myself 'I'm going to quit.' I put the pack in my pocket, and when I got home I wrote *'I quit!'* on the pack, dated it, and threw it on top of our kitchen cabinets."

True to his word, Tony never smoked a cigarette again. Many years later, Viola was out of cigarettes herself and climbed up onto the cabinets to retrieve the infamous package from 1959. She recalled the drastically expired cigarettes tasting horrible. The worst part of the ordeal was that Tony was the one who had taught her how to smoke in the first place.

By the mid-1960's, Tony was promoted to Sales Manager at the Blessings Corporation with responsibilities for the Nassau and Suffolk County regions of Long Island. The role had him splitting time between Long Island and Manhattan. He dedicated many hours over many years ensuring that his employees were properly trained and effective salespeople.

On December 1, 1980, Tony's loving mother Maria finally reunited with her husband Michael as she passed on from this earth. It was exactly thirty-nine years since that fateful month in 1941, when Japan attacked Pearl Harbor and Tony suffered the death of his father within a matter of weeks. Tony always lamented over not having done enough for his mother once he returned home safely from the war. He took her out to dinner every now and then, but regretted not doing more given that she was alone. They never did travel to Europe together as he had hoped for in his letters from England in 1944. However, Maria did travel to Italy on her own one August many years later. She sent her children and grandchildren a postcard of her smiling on a pier in Salerno. In reality, his mother was likely grateful for every moment she spent with him, and Tony was too self-critical given his high standards of affection as indicative in his letters during the war.

Tony shared that Maria had met someone in the early years when he first returned home from the war. The man was a nice Italian musician who lived in their neighborhood. The two would sit in the park and exchange pleasantries. One day Tony said to his mother lovingly, "Mom, you don't want to have to wash dirty socks and stuff again, do you?" Maria agreed and she never remarried. Her heart truly remained with her late husband, and she instead kept herself active in the lives of her four children and their families.

In 1982, Tony retired from the Blessings Corporation after nearly thirty years of service. His retirement, the absence of his mother, and his children's preoccupation with families of their own, led him to reconnect with his past military service in a more meaningful way. He began volunteering with his local Veterans of Foreign Wars (VFW) organization. He served as Junior Vice Commander for one year and Senior Vice Commander for another before being elected Commander in 1988. Leading his post for the next seven years, Tony significantly improved its stature in the community and financial health. He involved himself with the broader VFW at the county, district, and state levels, and was recognized for his success in member recruitment. He dedicated himself to the organization for ten years in all, volunteering at veterans hospitals, speaking at elementary schools, and even shoveling snow in the winter. He received numerous awards from the organization for his leadership. Perhaps the highest compliment received for his efforts came in a letter upon his retirement from the VFW in 1995, which said, "Without [Tony's] work, there would have been no Veterans Day celebration in Kings Park."

Aside from his commitment to the VFW, Tony also joined the Ninth Infantry Division Association, attending their annual reunions with Viola. The couple shared a story from one year in which they had an amusing interaction with General Westmoreland.[21] The general had just finished delivering a speech, and Tony approached the stage as conversation at the dinner tables resumed.

"Excuse me, General," Tony said pleasantly. "Can you do me a favor?" Everyone in my family is a veteran except for my wife," referring to himself and his two children.

"Well, how about we correct that?" replied Westmoreland. "Invite your better half to join us."

Viola came over and the general politely asked her to bow. He then said, "I bestow onto you, Mrs. Viola Varone, Honorary Sergeant Major to the outfit." The final piece was complete.

Such lighthearted memories were frequent at reunions. They served to offset some of the more serious sentiments that crossed Tony's mind when he reflected on his life and the war.

There was always a part of him that hoped that the memory of what he and his men achieved would not

---

[21] William C. Westmoreland served in the 34th Field Artillery Battalion of the 9th Infantry Division during World War II. He also served in the Korean War, and is most widely recognized as the commander of all U.S. forces during the Vietnam War, and the U.S. Army's Chief of Staff in its aftermath.

be forgotten. When the war ended, he questioned how their heroic accomplishments at Kasserine Pass, Le Desert, and other sacred battlegrounds were never fully recognized. Inquiring with a local Army office in 1945, he was told, "The war is over, pal. Forget about it." As he aged, and the flashbacks of combat replayed in his mind, he again reasoned that having formal medals that he might pass onto his children was a fair request in exchange for the sacrifices he made in the prime of his youth.

In his words, "I read some of the things about these other guys who got them, and I said 'Well I did more than that, and I didn't get anything.' I never wanted to brag while in service because the other men in my outfit told me, 'If you brag, we're going to lose you.' It meant that if I bragged about what I did to someone of importance, I could be transferred out of my platoon and sent to officer training. I think one of our guys took advantage of what we did in Kasserine and followed that path."

Years later, Tony happened to be visiting his nephew, who lived in Pennsylvania at the time, when he learned that a fellow veteran of the Ninth also lived in the area. It was the lieutenant who had written up Tony for his Bronze Star Medal for valor. The two men met at a hotel bar. The retired lieutenant brought a bottle of wine and offered Tony a drink. Tony declined; he had given up drinking years ago. Eventually the conversation turned to a dialogue with which Tony had grown familiar over the years.

"How many medals did you wind up with, Tony?" asked the lieutenant.

"Just one," said Tony, reciting his standard response.

Tony had received plenty of medals and decorations for his participation in campaigns, good conduct and meritorious service, and for honors bestowed upon his unit, but he understood the question being asked. The lieutenant was referring to medals associated with individual heroism, awarded to an individual soldier, such as the Bronze and Silver Star, the Medal of Honor, and the Purple Heart. For Tony, the sole medal that fell into that category was the Bronze Star for which the lieutenant had submitted the report.

"Geez!" replied the lieutenant. "I got two Silver Stars and the Purple Heart!"

Tony thought to himself how seldom the lieutenant had been on the front lines during the war. He did not hold anything against the man, but was reminded of how complex the recording of the actions of each and every soldier must have been amid the chaos of war, and how someone relatively lower in rank like

Tony was facing a reality of significantly lower odds that his actions would be properly recorded. He came to an understanding in that moment that medals would not alter the relevance and significance of the events in which he was involved. In those pivotal years of combat on behalf of the United States of America and its citizens, Tony's eyes had recorded all that he needed to be proud of his efforts. More medals would just be additional artifacts from events in a distant land and a time long ago, stored in that indistinct room to the left, on the second floor of his Kings Park home.

VFW Commander Varone at Nissequogue Post #5796.

50th Anniversary of D-Day
— June 6, 1994 —

Military Honors of
SGT. ANTHONY P. VARONE

- Bronze Star Medal
    - o "V" Device for Valor (Individual Heroism)
    - o 1st Oak Leaf Cluster (Meritorious Service)
    - o 2nd Oak Leaf Cluster (Citation in Orders)
- Presidential Unit Citation, Contenin Peninsula (1st Battalion)
    - o 4th Platoon (Anti-Tank Company) Attached
- Infantry Blue Cord
- Combat Infantryman Badge
- Good Conduct Medal
- American Defense Service Medal
- American Campaign Medal
- European-African-Middle Eastern Campaign Medal
    - o 1 Silver Service Star (5 Campaigns)
    - o 3 Bronze Service Stars (3 Campaigns)
    - o 1 Arrowhead Device (Amphibious Invasion)
- World War II Victory Medal
- Army of Occupation Medal
    - o Germany Clasp
- French Fourragère
- Belgian Fourragère
- Medal of a Liberated France
- Medal of Belgian Gratitude
- New York State Conspicuous Service Cross
    - o Awarded July 17, 1972 and February 10, 1997
- French Jubilee of Liberty Medal
    - o Awarded June 6, 1994 [50th Anniversary of D-Day]
    - o Received March 27, 1999
- Honor Flight to Washington D.C.
    - o Honored November 7, 2009
- Chevalier of the French Legion of Honor
    - o Awarded November 11, 2011 [Veterans Day]

CHAPTER THIRTEEN

Reflections

In 1941, the Army and Navy Publishing Company published the "Historical and Pictorial Review" of the 39th Infantry Regiment at Fort Bragg. Similar to a high school yearbook, the publication listed the names and portraits of each soldier by company, and summarized in words and photographs the experience of their training at Fort Bragg. Tony recently reviewed those many names and faces, sharing with reverence the variety of paths that their lives followed in the aftermath of those relatively simpler days in North Carolina.

What determined a soldier's survival? Was everything based on chance? Or was there skill involved? The answers to these complex questions are multifaceted. Some of those young men were killed in their very first moment of combat. On the other hand, one soldier was wounded on six separate occasions and kept returning to fight. He refused to go home until the war was over and received six Purple Hearts.

Other paths were less obvious. There was a sergeant who had repeatedly expressed his eagerness for combat while at Fort Bragg. In North Africa, he was assigned to clerical work at a command post far behind the front lines. He befriended the officers and believed that he had learned all he needed from them on how to lead other men and be successful in combat. When his command post received word that a higher-ranking officer had stepped on a mine and become disabled, the sergeant volunteered to replace the wounded officer. He was promoted and given leadership of his own unit in El Guettar. In his very first night of combat, he abandoned his men. Seizing a case of rations, he jumped into a jeep and headed back towards the command post without a word. He managed to avoid disciplinary action and was reassigned to the Army Post Office. For the remainder of the war, Tony's incoming mail from friends and family would occasionally have additional writing on the back of the envelope from this soldier:

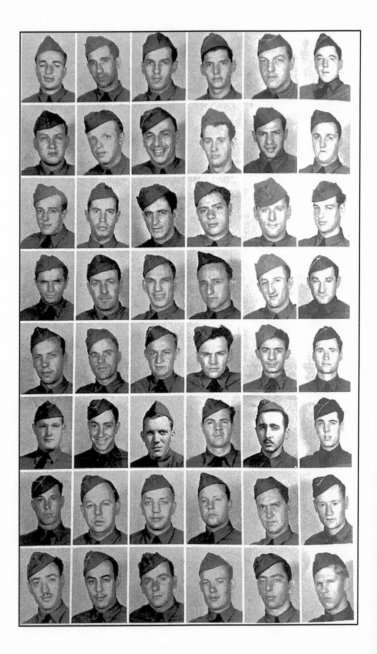

"Hope all is well, Tony! Miss you!" After the war, the former sergeant showed up at the radio store that Tony briefly owned. He apparently lived in the same neighborhood and had a broken radio in need of repair. Tony was at a loss for words.

While some soldiers fled in response to fear or fatigue, others remained despite being pushed to their psychological breaking point. One soldier who worked at headquarters was responsible for the transfer and guarding of German prisoners. His breakdown began as the Allies were crossing the Rhine. The stream of prisoners was incessant. Having to feed them and tend to their wounds while considering how many of his fellow men they may have killed on the battlefield became an increasingly stressful and conflicting set of circumstances.

Tony expounded on the path of one final soldier, albeit with a more solemn tone than he did the others. It was that of his friend Arty. The fiery spirit with whom Tony had formed uplifting memories at Fort Bragg went on to experience his own share of terrifying combat in North Africa. Tragically, Arty's psychological health severely deteriorated before the Allies were able to claim victory on the continent. He was found in a latrine attempting to end his life by slicing his wrists with a knife. He was caught in time to be rescued and was eventually sent home to the states with a bad conduct discharge. Years later, Tony travelled to upstate New York for a Veterans of Foreign Wars convention and looked Arty up in the phonebook. The two men had not seen each other since before the war in the Chesapeake Bay. They met for lunch and spent some quality time together. Tony noticed the scars on Arty's wrist from what happened in North Africa. He thanked Arty for everything he had taught him early on in their training at Fort Bragg. Although Arty may have succumbed to the darkest corners of war, Tony believed that Arty's guidance had helped save his life. Tony later remarked that stories like Arty's were regrettably not unique.

Mental fortitude was one of the most valuable weapons a soldier could have in his arsenal. It was the source of courage, effective decision-making, and resilience. Nevertheless, mental toughness could not protect a soldier from chance — those unfortunate circumstances of being ambushed by the enemy or placed in an impossible situation with severely limited odds of survival. Nor could it protect a soldier from incidents such as friendly fire. Thousands of powerful, destructive weapons in concentrated areas were destined to yield unintended consequences. Catastrophic events occurred from erroneous air and artillery strikes, as well as from the mishandling of smaller armed weapons. Tony recalled a sergeant accidentally blowing off his own hand while demonstrating a German bazooka to American troops in England. Someone had failed to tell the sergeant that the weapon was loaded.

Tony elaborated on this fragility of life from his perspective as a squad leader. In this role, he saw firsthand the constant stream of new recruits being sent over from the States to serve as replacements for the killed and wounded. Their level of training was severely lacking compared with those who had enlisted before the war. While soldiers like Tony had spent nearly two years at Fort Bragg, many of these young recruits joined the Army and were sent overseas within a couple of months.

In his words, "They came in for six weeks of training and were shipped out. Some didn't even write their names on a piece of paper yet. Guys would come up to me in the morning or evening and say, 'Hey Sergeant, I was told to report to you, I'm the new replacement.' And they would be killed the next morning. Sometimes I did not even know their names."

Leadership from superior officers helped foster individual psychological resilience. Similar to other social hierarchies, the perception that a higher-ranking officer was handling circumstances with composure could resonate with the lower ranks. The chain followed from the top to the bottom and helped maintain morale. In Tony's words, "I had to be [a role model], because if I got killed, somebody else would have to take over, and know what to do."

There is a repetition of battle that has been directly and indirectly alluded to several times amid these pages. It was entwined in the sheer length of the Second World War and the tedious number of consecutive months for which its participants served. There are stories that Tony shared which could not rightfully be included within his account of a particular campaign, because they were ubiquitous. They equated to the dismal and chilling routine that comprised the days and nights of Tony and the 4th platoon. They were perhaps more broadly indicative of the reasons that soldiers deserted or experienced mental breakdowns. They harbored the senseless, endless, and hideous nature of war in its truest form:

Soldiers were often killed and wounded by booby traps set by the enemy. Each time this occurred, Tony and his men would be tasked with locating and disabling the neighboring traps. They would creep along the ground searching for a range of devices. Some traps used transparent wires stretched a few inches off the ground that would detonate when a soldier stepped through the line. Others were activated when a soldier stepped on concealed prongs sticking up out of the ground. One device would shoot the explosive waist-high into the air before detonating lethal shrapnel in all directions.

The platoon spent evenings retrieving wounded men still lying on the ground from previous battles. They would attend to the men with medics who tried to patch them up. A pair from the platoon would then transport the wounded on stretchers. Sometimes the injuries sustained were too severe and resulted in immediate death. Other times death came slowly as aids looked on helplessly.

The already implicit brotherhood of the platoon could not have been better exemplified than when tasked with the duty of clearing an enemy minefield. Four or five men worked simultaneously to deactivate mines within a few feet of each other.

In Tony's words, "You have to trust the other guys, because if just one guy screws up, everyone is dead. During the day, the Germans fired machine guns and even sniper fire over a minefield to protect it. They tried to kill you so you fell on the mine and killed the men around you. So many guys were wounded. If you were careless for just a moment, or if you were beginning to get something into the pinhole and they fired near you and you messed up, your head would come right off. They wouldn't fire at night, but it was even harder then, because you couldn't see. I'm not sure which was worse."

By the war's end, Tony and the men beside him had successfully defused hundreds of enemy mines. Each mine posed an imminent threat to his life and the lives of his comrades. They could never become complacent and were required to treat each mine with the same exactitude. While Tony remained diligent in these and all technical matters related to combat, his overall mentality behind the precise motions of his body changed over time.

"I hardened," said Tony. "I didn't give a damn. I felt that I was going to get killed, so let me do the most damage I can to the enemy. It gets to that point where you don't always worry about how to protect yourself. You just say, 'The hell with it. They want to hit me, let them hit me, I'm just going to do what I have to do.'" The same attitude was applied to ensuring his proper rest: "I slept sitting up; I slept against trees; I slept with bullets flying around me."

Over time, some of Tony's pals facetiously called him the "bad penny," because no matter where he was ordered into battle, he kept coming back alive, like a penny that you attempt to discard but the person behind you picks it up and returns it. As the soldiers referred to his improbable survival in jest, Tony never had the slightest inclination for bravado. Instead, he became ever more grateful for each passing day.

In his words, "I always lived for today and not tomorrow, because I didn't know what was going to happen the next day. I never felt that I was going to live through it. I thought that I would definitely be killed. I could not understand how I kept coming out of these things alive. I was lucky spending so much time there, and coming back alright."

Variances of these routines and repetitions of war are relived deep in the souls of those elderly men in your neighborhoods, restaurants, and coffee shops who wear baseball caps adorned with the symbol "WWII". Tony never lost his positive spirit and exceptional sense of humor. He remained physically resilient throughout his life, the entry requirements for a man in his age bracket. He endured at least three heart attacks, two heart failures, nine hernias, and nearly a dozen operations.

"I think my wife and I got lucky," he said. "We're still around; ninety-three and ninety-five. We're not completely healthy, but we're not that bad."

Although he managed to maintain his physical health, Tony battled with emotional wounds for decades. "In my heart, I still miss the men I lost," he said nostalgically, as if the happier memories of those men flashed briefly across his mind. His eyes then glanced sadly towards the floor, suggesting those memories had been replaced by images concerning the circumstances of those soldiers' deaths; perhaps in part once the origin of his emotional struggles.

The room in Tony's home containing medals, memorabilia, and photographs, also contains the manuscripts and writings that helped make this book possible. They were compiled by Tony during many sleepless nights, over the course of those decades, and in some cases at the cost of significant pain and suffering. These stacks of paper filled with personal writings relived his most meaningful and powerful moments of the war, time and time and time again. He collected an abundance of newspaper clippings pertaining to soldiers who have been honored over the years for their service. He also collected stories concerning the terrible symptoms and experiences associated with a four-letter acronym that was not properly identified until decades after World War II: PTSD. Today, we have a better understanding of post-traumatic stress disorder and enhanced treatment methods. We can only hope for much greater progress to come.

The young soldier at war who managed to find the strength to consistently write to his friends and family that he was "in perfect health and feeling fine," was as we know experiencing a much more contrasting reality. Tony drafted the following note much later in life. The date is unspecified, however it captures the heart of the matter at hand:

"War is like a cancer – it eats away at me constantly. My emotions feel wounded beyond repair . . . Through the many battles, I prayed to get wounded or even killed, for I could hardly bear to get through another day of combat, to endure any more horrors of war where I would see so much death and pain and suffering.

"After I returned home from the war, I was treated at VA hospitals for battle fatigue and hypertension. At home I would be so upset that I would blow up and fly off the handle too easily. That hurt very much because I was doing it to those I love.

My mother suffered watching me go through those bad panic dreams. I was very restless and many nights I awoke from my sleep all sweaty – so much so that I had to change my sleepwear, pillow, and sheets. I tried to block out the memories of my buddies being killed and wounded, and how we carried on through heat; cold; hunger; rain; snow; death; injuries; sleepless

nights; long marches from place to place to close gaps;
the climb down the rope nets on the side of the ships to
get into the landing craft so that we could hit the
beaches; and then follow that by one hill after another
and one bridge after another; then one river after
another; and one invasion after another; and so on. It
was difficult for me to go to victory parades for fear of
seeing my deceased buddies go marching by."

Over the years, Tony regained peace within himself. He became an avid gardener, and found solace tending to his plants and working on projects around the house. He explored his artistic abilities and spent many hours writing down his thoughts and emotions. He never lost that sense of humor. He did everything he could to enjoy his bright marriage, life, and family.

"Viola has always been a wonderful wife and mother," he said. "She has always had a great desire to build strong ties with family, friends, and everyone in our community. She is a great person and I have been so lucky to have her in my life."

Similar to his years at combat, Tony managed to bend but not break. He achieved a state of mind that can best be exemplified in an exchange that occurred during the compilation of this book:

"Time heals all wounds they say," said Tony.

"You think it does?" asked Steven.

"Yeah, I think it does. Because as sad as I used to feel, about different things that happened to me in service, they finally shake off. You shake them out of your life. You persevere and go ahead, step ahead. There are some people who can't do it. They break up and they just can't get back into the swing of things. But you gotta make it, gotta make it! Gotta get back. Make the most of it."

War itself is not romantic, nor should it be glorified. However, the sacrifices of passing generations, those countless ordinary human beings like Tony who were placed by their will or the will of others into such inhuman circumstances, should be glorified. There are obvious and less obvious lessons to be learned from those who lived to tell their stories; characteristics of strength, gratitude, resilience, and humility that should be adopted and carried on by today's generation. Tony's is the story of an individual who persevered courageously through an incredible ordeal without ever being severely harmed. As he managed to remain untouched, so too were his heroics — Until now.

Tony and Viola.

– 1998 –

Tony at his home in Kings Park.

– January 2014 –

Acknowledgements

My sincerest thanks to all those who provided their time, support, and encouragement throughout the course of this endeavor, especially my loving parents, Jen, Seth, Mike, Tim, Eliot, and Kyle. Your kindness, generosity, and selflessness will always be remembered.

Thank you Tony, Viola, Michele, and Rick for allowing me into your lives, welcoming me into your homes, and entrusting me with this labor of love. It has been my greatest honor.

- Steven

About the Author

Steven Attanasio was born and raised in Brooklyn, New York. He is proud to be releasing his first book. Steven graduated from Cornell University's College of Arts & Sciences in 2008 where he earned a Bachelor of Arts in Government. After college, he worked in sales and trading at Goldman Sachs in New York for five years. He now lives and writes in New York City. He enjoys playing ice hockey and chess, and fostering his passion for travel, the exploration of new places, and the learning of new trades. He is an alumnus of Xaverian High School '04.

15514948R00136

Made in the USA
Middletown, DE
09 November 2014